Building Faith

LEADER'S GUIDE

Knowing Christ: believing
Growing in Christ: becoming
Reflecting Christ: being

Building Faith

LEADER'S GUIDE

Knowing Christ: believing
Growing in Christ: becoming
Reflecting Christ: being

Edited by
Ray E. Barnwell, Sr.

wesleyan
publishing
house

Indianapolis, Indiana

Contributing Writers and Editors

Ray E. Barnwell, Sr.
Robert Brown
Jerry Pence
Darlene Teague
Lawrence W. Wilson

Discipleship Project Committee

Earle L. Wilson, Chairman
Ray E. Barnwell, Sr., Project Director
Martha Blackburn
Dan Berry
Donald D. Cady
Ross DeMerchant
Steve DeNeff
James Dunn
Russ Gunsalus
Ron McClung
Robert E. Brown, Advisory Member
Darlene Teague, Advisory Member

Table of Contents

Preface

Welcome to the exciting journey of discipleship! This book—part of the *Building Faith* series—offers you a great opportunity to lead others in growing spiritually. In fact, the entire series has been developed for just that purpose—to help you shape the lives of others as disciples of Jesus Christ. By leading these studies, you will be helping others to live according to God's Word, using spiritual disciplines such as Bible study, prayer, fasting, Scripture memorization, meditation, and journal writing.

Discipleship is the continuing process of spiritual development. It begins at conversion and continues as long as we live—it's a lifelong journey. Discipleship takes place most effectively within an environment of belief—a safe place where people can grow in and learn to practice their faith.

One such environment is a Christian home, where a loving family helps each member discover and develop faith. The home is a place where faith is taught, modeled, and practiced. It is the place where most people experience unconditional love for the first time.

The Christian body—the church—is another environment where faith can be discovered and practiced. As in the home, relationships in the church are the key to spiritual growth. Christ referred to the church as His body, a place of connection, a place of belonging. The church is the only earthly institution that is focused fully on faith development.

Most of the new believers I speak with still have questions; they're looking for clarification. And they are longing for Christian relationships. Wouldn't it be great if there was a place they could go to make friends and find answers? Wouldn't it be wonderful if they could discover a forum to open their hearts, grow in the faith, and find unconditional love?

There is such a place!

Sunday School and other small group discipleship settings provide exactly that kind of environment for building faith. Discipleship moves beyond worship to involve people in building their faith in the context of loving relationships. Just as the New Testament church was built on teaching and preaching (Acts 5:42), so today's church must be built on Bible study. Gaining a thorough knowledge of the Bible is best done by participating in a Sunday

School class or Bible study group in addition to attending worship services. Both are important. One without the other can create an imbalance in your spiritual life. Being connected to a family-like unit that's relationship based is a vital component of discipleship.

In most churches, that caring, nurturing unit is called Sunday School. Other churches achieve this interaction through discipleship groups of various kinds. Whatever the name, day, or place of meeting, the fact is that everyone needs a protected environment in which to discover and practice the faith.

If you want to help others grow and become more effective in the Christian faith, urge them to join a Sunday School class or discipleship group.

Along with involvement in a discipleship class or small group, there are some other disciplines that have been proven to enhance spiritual formation. You can boost the your spiritual growth of your group members by inviting them to use these simple tools.

Bible Reading and Study. The *Building Faith* series is designed to direct you back to the Bible at every point in your study. Each chapter begins with one or two important Scripture passages and includes dozens of Bible references to explore. You can enhance your group's study of the Bible by using a good Bible translation, written in today's language, such as the New International Version (NIV).

Scripture Memorization. Memorization is a simple way to gain ownership of important Scripture verses. Each of the chapters in these books includes a key verse to memorize. At the end of the book is a Scripture memory tool—perforated flash cards containing the key verse for each chapter. Recommend that your group members memorize these verses; they'll gain confidence in their knowledge of Scripture.

Daily Prayer and Reflection. Time alone with God is perhaps the single most important spiritual practice for any disciple. Spend time in prayer and reflection every day, and ask your group members to do the same.

A Personal Spiritual Journal. Journal writing is a way to enhance time spent in prayer and reflection. Recording observations about life and faith will help disciples process what they are learning and clarify the spiritual issues in their lives. There is a personal spiritual journal page included in each chapter of the *Building Faith* books. At the end of each book is an extended journal section that may be used to expand journal writing. Invite your group members to make this study their opportunity to begin the practice of journal writing. They'll be glad they did.

All of these elements are designed to assist you in the journey of *Building Faith.*

Yours for Building People of Faith—

RAY E. BARNWELL, SR.

Getting Started

Understanding the *Building Faith* Approach

A new day is here for both new and existing believers. This new day is being driven by a fresh passion to make more and better disciples. And that fresh passion has given rise to a new system of values in the church. Instead of judging our success by measuring things—counting bodies, measuring buildings, and adding up "bucks"—we're focused on building faith. We want to make disciples who are devoted to knowing, loving, and serving Jesus Christ. All that we do to assist each believer is designed with the goal of growing people toward spiritual maturity—that is discipleship.

To do that, we need a *strategy* and a *process*.

The Strategy: Building People

The *Building People Strategy* is the basis of the *Building Faith* approach. Our disciple-making strategy rests upon four core values. They are:

- Sharing Love—Evangelism

- Shaping Lives—Discipleship

- Serving Like Christ—Ministering to Society

- Sending Leaders—Mobilization

Here's how it works: having discovered Christ, you will want to grow in your knowledge of Him—shaping your life according to God's Word. As you do, you will discover a personal ministry, a way to use your spiritual gifts to serve others. Then, having been filled with compassion for others, you will be moved to go into the world, fulfilling the Great Commission by evangelizing the lost—thus completing the cycle of discipleship.

The Process: Building Faith

We implement the *Building People* strategy through a process called *Building Faith*. *Building Faith* is a *competencies model*, meaning that it's focused on integrating important abilities into every aspect of a believer's life. These core competencies are organized around five categories:

- Biblical Beliefs

- Lifestyle Practices

- Virtues

- Core Values

- Mission

This process aims to form disciples according to the Great Commandment and the Great Commission.

The method is encapsulated in chart that follows. You'll want to bookmark this page and refer to it often.

Foundational Truths

Building Faith is based on ten foundational truths, which are key elements for life transformation. These biblical concepts encompass the scope of Christian thinking. Teaching these truths to new believers will help them grow in the faith. If you're a pastor, you might consider using these truths as the basis for worship and preaching during this study.

Practices

Every believer must move from theory to practice. That is, he or she must learn to apply biblical truth to life. The practices identified in *Building Faith* assist the believer to enact his or her faith and become life transformation.

Virtues

Virtues are Christlike qualities that emerge in the life of the believer, replacing sinful thoughts and attitudes. These virtues reveal the developing character of a transformed person and attract others to Christ. These virtues are also known as the *fruit of the Spirit.*

Core Values

Biblical truth must be applied in the framework of Christ's body, the church. The core values are the guiding principles by which our church functions. They are our method of operating, describing *how* we do the things we do.

Mission

Ultimately, believers are called to serve. The mission describes what it is that we do for Christ. Each biblical truth finds a practical expression in our work.

As you make more and better disciples, the *Building Faith* series will aid you in making believers higher, deeper, fuller, and freer in Christ's love.

Building Faith				
Foundational Beliefs	**Lifestyle Practices**	**Personal Virtues**	**Core Value**	**Mission**
The Trinity	Worship	Joy	Biblical Authority	Discipling Believers
Salvation by Grace	Prayer and Faith	Peace and Grace	Biblical Authority	Evangelizing the Lost
Authority of the Bible	Practicing the Mind of Christ and Discipline	Faithfulness	Biblical Authority	Discipling Believers; Equipping the Church
Personal Relationship with God	Bible Study and Prayer	Self-Control	Christlikeness; Disciple-Making	Discipling Believers
Identity in Christ	Baptism, Lord's Supper	Humility and Grace	Local Church Centered	Discipling Believers
Church/ Family of God	Biblical Community of Faith Beginning in a Christian Home	Love	Local Church Centered; Servant Leadership	Ministering to Society; Discipling Believers
Eternity/Global Evangelism	Lifestyle Evangelism	Love and Obedience	Disciple-Making; Unity in Diversity	Evangelizing the Lost
Stewardship (Including Good Works, Compassion)	Making Christ Lord of Time, Money, Life	Humility, Patience and Goodness	Disciple-Making; Servant Leadership	Equipping the Church; Ministering to Society
Freedom of the Will	Biblical World View	Obedience	Cultural Relevance; Biblical Authority	Discipling Believers; Equipping the Church
Holiness	Godliness, Loving Obedience to God's Revealed Will	Patience, Gentleness, Kindness, Love	Christlikeness; Disciple-Making	Discipling Believers; Ministering to Society

Making the Most of These Sessions

Session Design

Each session is designed around six segments, each with a specific goal. Knowing that the length of your sessions may vary, we have not suggested a minimum or maximum time to be spent on each activity; however, we strongly recommend that the majority of your time be spent in the *Discovering* and *Observing* segments.

Here's a snapshot of the six elements of each session.

Connecting

The purpose of the *Connecting* segment is to help your group members develop a bond with one another. Group leaders and teachers sometimes try to deliver content before connecting to the students. That's a mistake. Your group's ability to learn will be enhanced by this segment: it sets the stage for the entire session.

To create openness among your members, try using the *kitchen* style class. When you think of a kitchen, you picture people sitting around a table, usually eating, with laughter, talking, and lots of interaction. The kitchen is an informal setting where people really enjoy themselves. That's the atmosphere you'll want to create for this group: a protected environment of love and acceptance where faith can be discovered and practiced.

Use the connecting time to lead your group in a time of sharing, caring, and praying.

Sharing. This may include an icebreaker, which leads to a time when people share a concern, need, or prayer request. (Some icebreaker activities are provided later in this chapter.)

Caring. Caring builds on the sharing time by allowing people to help one another deal with problems or concerns. That may take the form of offering help, encouragement, or support. Caring also takes place outside of the meeting time through acts of kindness offered by group members to each other. You'll want to model this caring and may need to suggest ideas for caring to your group.

The next week, you may want to check on the concerns that were raised. That will hold members accountable for the support they offer and ensure that no one is forgotten.

Praying. Finally, pray together about the needs and concerns of the group. There's more than one way of praying as a group. You might have one person pray for the group, ask a different person to pray for each need, break into groups of two or three where each person can pray for the others, or pray silently. Vary the prayer methods that you use, and be sure to spend at least half of your prayer time on spiritual needs.

Discovering

The next segment of your meeting is *Discovering* or Bible study time. A major focus of the *Building Faith* series is teaching the Bible.

As the leader, your role in helping students discover the truth is critical. Spend adequate time in personal preparation so that you'll be familiar with the Scripture for that session. Your personal connection to God and His Word will enable you to teach others effectively.

Encourage group members to bring a Bible with them. Each chapter of each *Building Faith* book is loaded with Bible references. Ask students to look up some of the references, and use the *Connecting God's Word to Life* section of each chapter as a lead-in to Bible study.

Memorizing

Biblical illiteracy is at an all-time high, even among church attendees. Help your students hide God's Word in their hearts by helping them memorize Scripture.

Each chapter contains a memory verse. There are a number of Scripture memorization techniques you can use with your group. Several are included later in this chapter.

Observing

Observing is the heart of your teaching time. This is where you will help students understand the two or three key concepts of the lesson. It's likely that there will be more ideas than you can thoroughly explore during your session time. Don't let that frustrate you. Personalize the material to meet your group's needs. You may find that the group members already have a handle on some of the important concepts. That will allow you to spend more time elsewhere. By giving yourself adequate preparation time, you'll be able to personalize and adapt the lesson to meet your group's need.

Be sure to draw from you own experiences and insights when leading the group. Be transparent. Remember more is *caught* than *taught*!

Practicing

This element of your session is aimed at helping students apply the ideas that they've learned. It gives the group a chance to think about how to translate the ideas into their lives in practical ways. For the most part, they'll actually practice (that is, apply to life) these concepts outside the group meeting time.

Each chapter contains questions that call for the readers to think about how to apply what they're learning. You can use these questions to stimulate discussion during your meetings.

You may want to take time each week to see what actions group members took as a result of their learning. The *Connecting* segment of your group meeting is a good place to ask some accountability questions.

Closing

Closing is the element of your session that "brings it home," leading the group members to make a resolve or commitment based on their learning. Here is where you can summarize the ideas that you've discovered and ask students what "next step" they will take as a result of what they have discovered.

Encourage group members to prepare for the next session by reading the next chapter and practicing the simple disciplines that will make it more valuable: Bible study and memorization, daily prayer, and journal writing.

End the session time in a way that affirms what you've learned together and the resolves that students are making. You might choose to close with a prayer, a song, or an affirmation similar to the benedictions that are used at the close of a worship service.

Icebreakers

During the *Connecting* segment of your meetings, you'll want to use a variety of techniques to help group members interact with each other. Here are a few choices.

Getting to Know You

Ask group members to take turns introducing themselves. You might suggest one or two details for everyone to share, such as what school they attended, what they do, a hobby, their favorite food, or their hero. You can use this icebreaker more than once with the same group as long as you choose different details each time.

Introductions

Have group members pair up and interview one another. Then have each person introduce his or her partner to the group. Allow two to three minutes for the interviews. You might want to provide something to write on and direct their thinking with questions like: What's your favorite color? Where did you grow up? Do you have a pet? What's your favorite flavor of ice cream?

My Worst Moment

Ask for volunteers to share their most embarrassing or hilarious vacation experience. Other "worsts" that make interesting icebreakers include:

- Christmas gift
- Birthday gift
- Family reunion
- Embarrassing situation

This icebreaker may be used more than once as long as you use a different topic each time.

Same Letter Descriptions

Ask group members to introduce themselves using an adjective starting with the first letter of their last name. Example: "I am Sweet Smith."

Another version of this introduction game is to tell something you like that starts with the same letter of your first name. For example, "I'm Rhonda and I like rock climbing."

The Most Exciting

Ask members to share their most exciting moment. It might be an event, holiday, graduation, or accomplishment.

Guess Who I Am

Distribute cards and ask each member to record basic information about him- or herself, such as place of birth, school attended, or hobby, but not their names. Scramble the cards and redistribute them, asking each person to identify the person described on their card.

Find Someone Who—

Make a list of facts to discover about people. Include things like "Favorite color is blue," "Has a pet bird," "Has visited a mission field," or "Was on the homecoming court." Depending on the size of your group, you may want to list up to a dozen different things. Have group circulate to find out who (if anyone) fits the descriptions listed.

Name Tag Pictures

Ask each person to draw a picture of something that represents them or something they like. For example, someone who likes to restore old cars may draw a car on his or her name tag. Spend some time letting the group members ask each other what their name tag represents.

Secret Pals

Assign a secret pal for each group member (one of the other members of the group). Each person will do something special for his or her secret pal during the month. At the end of that time, members reveal the name of their secret pal. Some things to do for a secret pal:

- Send a card

- Give a small gift

- During class, serve your pal refreshments (you might serve a few other people, too, so it's not obvious who your pal is).

- Pray regularly for your pal

Remember, names should not be revealed until the end of the month so that everyone can have fun guessing the identity of his or her secret pal.

Meal Deal

Everyone seems to relax and enjoy conversation while eating. Find occasions for your group to eat together, even if it's only a snack. You might bring in finger foods to share during the meeting or desserts to share afterward. You might even have a pitch-in meal as part of your session, or go out to eat together.

Leader's Toolbox

Open a carpenter's toolbox, and you will see hammers, saws, chisels, and other tools. Look into a plumber's toolbox, and you will find wrenches, pipe cutters, torches, and the like. Each trade requires its own specialized equipment.

Now, open your leader's toolbox. What tools do you have for building people with the Word of God?

Remember that the *way* a lesson is taught significantly impacts *what* is learned. Wise teachers accumulate a number of tools to cultivate curiosity, communicate content, evoke emotions, prompt participation, inspire insight, fortify faith, and bolster behavior. Some are old standbys—timeless basics you can almost always count on to get the job done. Others are recent innovations made possible by new technology or the latest research.

Most of us who enjoy teaching are always on the lookout for fresh ideas as well as ways to keep the "old faithfuls" sharp. Here is a variety of teaching methods that you can add to your tool collection.

Interactive Methods

Question and Answer. Sometimes called the *Socratic method,* in this technique the teacher challenges learners by posing questions. There are three basic types of questions.

- *Factual questions* require the student to answer with specific information.

- *Thought questions* cause students to identify causes or solutions for certain situations. They are usually introduced with *how* or *why*.

- *Rhetorical questions* do not require an audible answer and are useful for emphasizing a truth or making a fact self-evident.

Forum. A forum is an open discussion or question and answer time under the direction of a moderator. This is especially useful following a presentation such as a lecture, interview, film, or symposium.

Group Discussion. In a group discussion, everyone works together to identify a truth or solution to a problem under the direction of a leader. The leader must be prepared to introduce the subject, keep the discussion on track, and summarize the conclusions at the end.

Buzz Groups. Buzz groups are smaller groups that simultaneously discuss the subject, often reporting conclusions to the larger assembly at the end.

Dyads and Triads. Dyads, sometimes called "neighbor nudging," are discussion groups of two. Triads are simply groups of three. Both allow for intimate personal sharing and are useful for involving everyone in a discussion.

Panel Discussion. A panel is a semistructured discussion in which three or four persons are chosen to represent different points of view. The discussion is guided by a moderator, who summarizes conclusions at the end.

Personal Participation Methods

Interview. Interviews are live conversations that allow the class to benefit from expert observations, real-life experiences, or insights from someone with specialized knowledge of a subject.

Silent Reflection. Invite students to think about a passage, about a question, or about their reactions or observations concerning a clearly stated problem. Prohibit members from speaking for a minute or two so that early reactors don't dominate the thinking of others.

Charts. Charts are useful to compare and contrast characteristics of Bible characters, teachings, or events; create lists of observations about a text; summarize lesson points; or simplify complex or long passages of Scripture.

Contests and Games. Bring out the child in every adult by creating your group's own version of a parlor game or a television game show that uses Bible characters and terms as clues or answers.

Direct Presentation Methods

Resource Person. A resource person is a guest presenter who is invited to share information or experiences directly related to the topic being studied by your class or group. The presentation becomes the basis for dialogue between group members or the guest and the group.

Object Lesson. Almost any physical prop can be used as a visual or sensory tool to reinforce the point of a lesson. An object lesson differs from a demonstration in that a demonstration is an illustration of a process or event, while an object lesson uses a prop as a metaphor to compare or contrast two things.

Debate. Two or more speakers alternately express their points of view (usually one pro and one con) about a proposition or issue. Each side has a chance to rebut the other's statements.

Storytelling. Storytelling is one of the most ancient means of teaching, in which an illustration, a real-life situation, an imaginary scenario, a historical incident, or a personal experience is recounted verbally. Stories are usually used for illustrative purposes and should shed light on the subject at hand. To be effective, they must be action oriented and told naturally, with enthusiasm, good vocal expression, appropriate gestures, and facial expressions.

Testimony. A testimony is a variation of the storytelling technique in which someone provides a firsthand, eyewitness account of a specific experience. It can be impromptu (just ask if someone in the class can verify a point made in the lesson from his or her experience) or extemporaneous (ask someone ahead of time to prepare to speak to a topic).

Team Teaching. In team teaching, two or more people take turns presenting lesson content (a bit like tag-team wrestling). For example, one person may present a mini-lecture, followed by a response or questions by the other; then another mini-lecture, after which the partner may lead a group discussion. Or a team-taught lesson may be presented by teachers carrying on a dialogue with each other about a text, and one or the other of them occasionally engaging the whole class in learning activities that invite their participation in the conversation.

Audiovisual Presentations. Chalkboards, maps, bulletin boards, pictures, charts, overhead projectors, cassettes, CDs, and computer graphics are just a few audiovisual aids teachers can use to communicate and illustrate information. Most of these, however, as suggested by the word *aids*, are used to augment another direct presentation technique. More and more resources are now available that use audiovisual means to present a wide variety of material. Technology can never replace the benefit of direct personal reflection and discussion in your class.

Direct Bible Study Methods

Group Observation. Observation simply means helping a group discover what the Bible says, before concluding what it means.

Cross Referencing. This technique seeks insight on a passage by looking for other texts that provide additional background information or restate it in another author's words.

Survey Method. A whole paragraph, section, or chapter (rather than a single verse) is taken as the basic unit of study.

Creative and Artistic Methods

Role-Playing. This time-honored technique allows students to act out a Bible story, a hypothetical situation, or interpersonal relationship.

Singing. Choose familiar tunes within easy voice range for most class members. Or invite a soloist to sing to your group.

Writing Assignments. Poems, limericks, short stories, testimonies, letters, sentences, paragraphs, journals, letters to imaginary editors, or articles are valuable expressions of new ideas, insights, and reflection.

Sculpting. Give group members a lump of Play Dough™ or modeling clay and invite them to illustrate something significant from the Bible passage your group is studying.

Memory Verse Learning Methods

Many adults believe they cannot memorize Scripture because their "memory is not what it used to be." In fact, anybody can memorize Bible verses with the aid of some simple techniques. Try these methods with your group members.

Memory Verse Envelope

Put each word of a memory verse on a separate piece of paper. Mix the pieces of paper and put them into an envelope. Make up enough envelopes to give one to each person or pair of people in your group. All the envelopes could contain the same verse or different verses. The first person or pair to put the words of the memory verse in the correct order is the winner.

Memory Verse Card Drill

On a piece of cardboard or construction paper, write the first half of a memory verse. Create several different cards, each with the beginning of a different verse. Hold a card for the group, and the first person to finish the memory verse (and give the verse reference) is the winner. A variation is to put memory verse references on the cards and have group members race to recite the verse correctly.

Push Pin Review

Have each word of a memory verse written on a three-by-five-inch card or piece of paper. Put up the cards in an incorrect order, and then have group members take turns putting the cards in the right order.

Memory Verse Match

Write a complete memory verse and reference on several cards, then cut the cards into two pieces so that the reference and half of the verse are on one side and the rest of the verse is on the other. Put the cards into a pile and have each person draw one piece of a card. When you give the signal, have the people try to find their "match."

You could make this a little more difficult by writing the verses incorrectly so that the group members would have to correct the mistakes after matching the two halves of the card.

Clue Word Memory Cards

Think of three to five words to serve as clues for a memory verse. Write each clue word on a separate card. Number the cards, with the number one indicating the most difficult clue, and the highest number indicating the least difficult. Divide the class into two groups. Show one group only the most difficult clue. If no one from that group can

BUILDING FAITH LEADER'S GUIDE

recite the verse, show the clue to the other group. If the other group cannot recite the verse on the first clue, go back to the first group and give them the second clue. Keep doing this until the memory verse is correctly recited, and give the card to the group that recited the verse. The group with the most cards at the end of the game wins.

A variation would be to assign a point value to each clue. For instance, if a group gets the verse right on the first clue, they get ten points; second clue, eight points; third clue, six points; fourth clue, four points; and fifth clue, two points. The first group to get fifty points would be the winner.

Whiteboard Verse

Write the memory verse on the whiteboard. Have the group, or each person individually, read the verse. Then erase a letter or word. Have the person recite the verse again as though the missing letters or words were still there. Continue to do this until all of the words are gone, having each person or the group continue to say the verse.

Guess a Letter

Draw a blank line for each letter in a memory verse. Ask one person to guess a letter. If that letter is in the verse, write it in the appropriate blank(s). Allow the person to keep guessing letters until he or she guesses incorrectly. You could modify this game by letting the group guess individual words. When they guess correctly, fill in the entire word wherever it appears in the verse. You might also write the verse reference on the board above the blanks for the verse or make the reference part of the puzzle. The first person to say the entire verse correctly wins.

Round Table Memory

Have the group sit in a circle. Write the memory verse on a board where it can be easily seen. Assign one word of the memory verse to each person in the group, then start at the beginning of the verse and have each person say his or her assigned word in turn to complete the verse. Gradually increase speed so that the group must recite the verse faster and faster. At some point, remove the board so that the group must recite the verse from memory.

A variation of this game is to have the first person in the circle say the first word of the verse, the second person say the first two words of the verse and so on until someone repeats the entire verse from memory.

Knowing Christ

believing

Session Plans

Knowing Christ

Leader's Introduction

Everything has a beginning: the world, each day, every person, even your students' faith in Christ. When your students became believers in Christ, their lives had new beginnings. As Jesus said, they were "born again." If you have new converts, be sure to welcome them to the family of God.

As part of God's family, your students are His children and He is their Father. And just as every earthly father wants to see his children grow, the Heavenly Father wants to see them mature also. Their growth and development are foremost in His mind. He wants them to become more and more like Him.

Your students may be thinking, "Me? Be like God? That's not possible!"

Yes, it is possible. They can grow to become the godly person that He wants them to be. You have the opportunity to help them grow. Of course, it won't happen overnight. Their development involves more than a single moment of decision or one week's church attendance. It's a process, a lifelong journey. That journey is called discipleship and you are here to help guide them.

Their journey began with their decision to follow Christ, and it has led them to this book, *Knowing Christ: believing,* a part of the *Building Faith* series. This unique series of books is designed to help people grow in the faith. It has been written with your students in mind. We are honored to welcome them and you on this journey.

Important spiritual guides on your students' journey will include the pastor, Sunday School teachers or small group leaders, Christian relatives and friends, perhaps a mentor or an accountability partner, and you the leader. They may be asking why they need all these people on their journey. Remember that Satan, the enemy of the soul, uses a variety of weapons to dampen faith. Right now, their faith is strong, like a hot fire. Satan will try to drown it out. One way of doing that is to isolate them from other believers. When you remove a single log from a fire, it soon goes out. But when several logs burn together, they fuel one another. In the same way, we all need other Christians in order to keep our faith burning brightly.

This book will also feed their faith in Christ. Each of your group members need a copy of the book. We hope they'll read it carefully. Be sure they read the introduction. It will help them make the most of this book. Help them think of it as a backpack filled with the supplies they'll need for a day's hike.

Here's a snapshot of what's ahead in *Knowing Christ: believing.*

Chapter one is about spiritual formation. It will show them how to grow as a new believer. It provides an overview of the journey and some of the equipment they will need to make it all the way.

The second chapter will help them understand what happened when they made their personal decision to follow Christ. It will also help them respond to others when they ask, "What's different about you?"

Chapter three is focused on the importance of the Bible in their new life. They will learn how to choose a version of the Bible, how to study it, and how to apply biblical principles to life.

They'll discover the importance of sharing their newfound faith in Christ in chapter four. They will learn why it's so important to tell this story and how to go about it.

The fifth chapter explores the deeper life that's possible for every Christian. They will learn what it means to be holy and how you can be holy too.

Many people first learn about God through a worship service. In chapter six they will explore the meaning and practice of Christian worship.

Life is a gift from God, and chapter seven shows the importance of managing that sacred trust wisely. They'll discover how to live a life that shows respect for God in the use of time, abilities, and resources.

The concluding chapter shows the importance of having healthy Christian relationships.

Once again, welcome! I'm glad you're helping others along on the journey of *Building Faith.*

RAY E. BARNWELL, SR.

CHAPTER 1

Growing in Your New Life

Spiritual Formation

Focus

This session explores the concept of spiritual formation, discovering the sources of truth God uses to reveal Himself and the way He works within us to transform us into His image, especially through daily prayer and Bible study.

Since the concept of spiritual formation is foundational to the *Building Faith* approach, this chapter is especially important. You may want to divide the chapter into two sessions, using the first session to talk about the concept of formation and the sources of truth God uses to form us and the second session to begin exploring the components of a daily quiet time with God.

Discovery: God intends to transform each believer into a new person.

Preparing

- ❏ Read chapter 1 of *Knowing Christ: believing.*
- ❏ Review Gal. 4:19; Eph. 4:14–15 and Rom. 12:2. Also read Eph. 4:11-16; 1 Pet. 2:2-3; and Phil. 2:12-13, noting the ways that Christ is formed within us.
- ❏ Review the Observing section of this lesson to identify the concepts that you will lead your group to discover.
- ❏ Choose an activity from "Icebreakers."
- ❏ Choose a teaching method from "Leader's Toolbox" that will help your group arrive at the discovery for this session.
- ❏ Choose a learning activity from "Memory Verse Learning Methods."
- ❏ Gather the materials you'll need for this session.

❏ Pray that God will use this study to transform lives.

Hint: Remember to vary your teaching methods from week to week. You can also use more than one method in a single session.

Suggested Object Lesson: Play-Doh

Bring enough Play-Doh for each person to create an object. Make the point that God has a plan in mind for our spiritual formation.

Suggested Songs

"Change My Heart, O God" (Eddie Espinosa); "Have Thine Own Way, Lord" (Adelaide A. Pollard); "Spirit of the Living God" (Daniel Iverson).

Connecting

Greet each member of your group and welcome them to the *Building Faith* series. Explain that the purpose of these sessions is to *help believers grow* in their new life in Christ.

People need to warm up to each other before they'll share the important things in their lives, so use one or more icebreaker activities to encourage relationship building.

If this group has met before and has already established relationships, continue the sharing, caring, and prayer time, using a variety of approaches.

If this group has not met together before, tell them that prayer, caring, and sharing each other's concerns will be an important part of what they do together. Invite group members to share:

- Praise Items—Good things that God has done in their lives lately

- Prayer Requests—Concerns for themselves or for a friend

- Needs—Things in their lives or in the community that the group might be able to help with

Consider enlisting someone to record prayer requests and praise items for the group each week—that will help you remember to pray consistently for important needs and celebrate answers to prayer.

Lead the group in a time of prayer. Remember, there are lots of ways for a group to pray together. See the "Leader's Toolbox" for some ideas.

Discovering

Review the important Scriptures for this session, giving special attention to those portions in italics. The key verse is printed in bold. Before you begin, ask the group, "What does it mean that Christ is formed in us." Throughout the session, focus on the aspect of developing a *relationship* with God, which—like any relationship—requires time and commitment.

Galatians 4:19

> My dear children, for whom I am again in the pains of childbirth until Christ is *formed* in you . . .

Ephesians 4:14–15

> ¹⁴Then we will no longer *be infants*, tossed back and forth by the waves, and *blown here and there by every wind of teaching.* . . . ¹⁵Instead, *speaking the truth in love*, we will in all things *grow up into him* who is the Head, that is, Christ.

Romans 12:2

> **Do not c*onform* any longer to the *pattern* of this *world*, but be *transformed* by the *renewing of your mind*. Then you will be able to *test* and *approve* what *God's will* is—his good, pleasing and perfect will.**

Memorizing

Lead your group in memorizing Rom.12:2, using one of the activities from "Memory Verse Learning Methods." Encourage the group to review the memory verses between sessions by using the flash cards printed at the end of *Knowing Christ: believing.* You may also want to encourage them to memorize by offering a gift to everyone who memorizes all the verses.

Observing

The key points to observe in this session are:

- *Spiritual formation* means changing and being changed into the image of Christ.

- The sources of God's truth are Scripture, reason, tradition, and experience.

- Daily time with God is essential for spiritual formation. That includes:

  Scripture—reading, meditating on, studying, and memorizing the Bible

  Prayer—talking to God, listening to God, and receiving guidance from the Holy Spirit.

Practicing

Challenge the members of your group to establish a daily time of prayer and Bible study this week. Consider inviting each person to partner with another to share their personal action plans for creating a devotional time and to pray together.

Closing

As you bring your class to a close by singing together the prayer chorus "Spirit of the Living God" or another song that speaks of being formed by God.

Affirm your willingness to be shaped by God as He transforms you into the likeness of Christ.

Before you dismiss:

- Remind group members to bring a Bible to each session of *Building Faith*.

- Encourage group members to continue their spiritual journey by joining a Sunday School class or small group.

- Say, "Next week, we will look at what happened when you were saved. You will discover how salvation affects us now and throughout eternity!"

CHAPTER 2

Understanding What God Did for You

Salvation

Focus

This session helps believers understand what God did for them when they put their faith in Jesus Christ. It explores the problem of sin, our inability to save ourselves, God's plan to provide salvation through Jesus Christ, and the forgiveness, pardon, and new birth that result from our faith in Christ.

Discovery: You can know that you have become a new person through faith in Christ.

Preparing

❏ Read chapter 2 of *Knowing Christ: believing.*

❏ Review Acts 16:29–31; John 3:3, 16; Rom. 5:1–2; and Titus 3:5 and note your personal insights.

❏ Review the Observing section of this lesson to identify the concepts that you will lead your group to discover.

❏ Choose an activity from "Icebreakers."

❏ Choose a teaching method from "Leader's Toolbox" that will help your group arrive at the discovery for this session.

❏ Choose a learning activity from "Memory Verse Learning Methods."

❏ Gather the materials you'll need for this session.

❏ Pray for each member of your group by name.

Hint: Some group members may be more comfortable writing their reactions than speaking aloud in class.

Suggested Object Lesson: A Cross

Bring a small cross to class and ask, "Where might you find a cross? What does the cross represent to you?" Explain that this session will explore reasons why the cross is important to our lives.

Suggested Songs

Amazing Grace" (John Newton); "Lord, I Lift Your Name on High" (Rick Founds).

Connecting

Use an icebreaker activity to encourage relationship building.

As a follow-up of the discussion on spiritual formation, you might invite group members to talk in pairs about their practice of Bible reading and prayer.

Invite group members to share:

- Praise Items—Good things that God has done in their lives lately

- Prayer Requests—Concerns for themselves or for a friend

- Needs—Things in their lives or in the community that the group might be able to help with

Review prayer requests from the last session, and lead the group in a time of prayer. Remember, there are lots of ways for a group to pray together. See the "Leader's Toolbox" for some ideas.

Discovering

Review the important Scriptures for this session, giving special attention to those portions in italics. The key verse is printed in bold. Before you begin, ask, "What happened when you were saved?" Point out that the Bible describes what God does for us when we believe in Christ.

Acts 16:29–31

29The jailer called for lights, rushed in, and fell trembling before Paul and Silas. 30He then brought them out and asked, "Sirs, *what must I do to be saved?"* 31They replied, *"Believe in the Lord Jesus, and you will be saved*—you and your household."

John 3:3

"I tell you the truth, unless a man is *born again*, he cannot see the *kingdom of God.*"

John 3:16

For *God so loved the world* that He gave His *one and only Son*, that whoever *believes in Him* shall not perish but have *eternal life.*

Romans 5:1–2

¹Therefore, since we have been *justified through faith*, we have *peace with God* through our Lord Jesus Christ, ²through whom we have *gained access into this grace* in which we now stand. And we rejoice in the *hope of the glory of God.*

Titus 3:5

He saved us, not because of righteous things we had done, but *because of His mercy.* He saved us through the *washing of rebirth* and *renewal by the Holy Spirit.*

Acts 4:12

Salvation is found in no one else*, for there is *no other name* under heaven given to men by which *we must be saved.

Ask students to write their answers to these questions, then share their responses with the group.

- What do these Scriptures tell you about salvation?

- How is it possible for you to be saved?

- In what ways do these verses help you understand what it means to be saved?

Throughout this session emphasize that there is only one way to have peace with God: through Jesus Christ our Lord.

Memorizing

Lead your group in memorizing Acts 4:12, using one of the activities from "Memory Verse Learning Methods." Remind your group that memorized Scripture is a Bible that can be taken anywhere. Encourage students to utilize the Scripture memory cards at the back of their book.

Observing

The key points to observe in this session are:

- The reason that we need to be saved is that we have sinned and are under the penalty of death.

- We may be saved by faith in Jesus Christ, God's Son.

- When we accept Christ as Savior, we are forgiven and reborn for a new life.

- We can be sure that we are saved by the authority of God's Word and by the confirmation of the Holy Spirit within our heart.

Practicing

Challenge group members to "tell their story," that is, to tell someone else about how they came to believe in Jesus Christ. Invite them to write the names of ten people whom they'd most like to tell about their faith, and to identify the person whom they will tell first. (You might suggest they use the "Ten Most Wanted" card. This resource is available from Wesleyan Publishing House.) Pray that God will open the way for them to tell their story to at least one person this week.

Closing

Bring your class to a close by offering a prayer, singing a song, or offering an affirmation and blessing.

Before you dismiss:

- Encourage group members to make use of the Personal Spiritual Journal pages included in each chapter of *Knowing Christ: believing*.

- Say, "Next week, we'll find out how we got the Bible—and how to use it!"

CHAPTER 3

Knowing God through His Word

Scripture

Focus

This session is about the Bible, our authoritative source of truth. This chapter first identifies the reasons we believe the Bible is inspired. Second, it shows how to study the Bible, answering several common questions about the Bible's origins and purpose.

Discovery: We can know God by knowing the Bible.

Preparing

❑ Read chapter 3 of *Knowing Christ: believing.*

❑ Study 2 Tim. 3:14–17. Notice key words and ideas.

❑ Review the Observing section of this lesson to identify the concepts that you will lead your group to discover.

❑ Choose an activity from "Icebreakers."

❑ Choose a teaching method from "Leader's Toolbox" that will help your group arrive at the discovery for this session.

❑ Choose a learning activity from "Memory Verse Learning Methods."

❑ Gather the materials you'll need for this session.

❑ Pray for your spiritual growth as you lead others in *Building Faith.*

Hint: Many people are visual learners. Consider using a prop or visual aid in this session.

Suggested Object Lesson: Bibles

Gather as many different versions of the Bible as you can find. As you open the *Discovering* portion of this session, say, "Today we're going to see why knowing God's Word is so important for a believer."

Suggested Songs

"Thy Word Is a Lamp Unto My Feet" (Michael W. Smith); "Wonderful Words of Life" (Philip Paul Bliss); "Open My Eyes that I May See" (Clara H. Scott).

Connecting

Use the icebreaker to encourage group members to share with one another. Then take a minute to encourage group members to talk about how they are applying the lessons of *Building Faith* to their personal lives. Allow time for responses. Review prayer concerns from the last session and invite the group to share new requests for prayer. Lead the group in praying together.

Hint: Remember that group interaction begins prior to the session itself. That's why room arrangement is important and a circle arrangement is often best.

Discovering

Review the important Scriptures for this session, giving special attention to those portions in italics. The key verse is printed in bold. Before you begin, ask, "What does it mean that the Bible is God's Word?"

2 Timothy 3:14–17

¹⁴But as for you, *continue in what you have learned* and have become convinced of, because you know those from whom you learned it, ¹⁵and how from infancy you have known *the holy Scriptures*, which are *able to make you wise for salvation* through faith in Christ Jesus. ¹⁶All **Scripture is God-breathed** and is **useful for teaching, rebuking, correcting and training** in righteousness, ¹⁷**so that the man of God may be** *thoroughly equipped for every good work*.

To help your group process these Scriptures, ask:

• What do these Scriptures tell us about the Bible?

- What value do they place on learning and applying the truths of the Bible?

- Why do (or don't) you believe the Bible is God's written Word?

Memorizing

Lead your group in memorizing 2 Tim. 3:16–17, using one of the activities from "Memory Verse Learning Methods." Remind group members that memorizing God's Word builds their strength to resist temptation and helps them make choices that please God.

Observing

The key points to observe in this session are:

- We know that the Bible is inspired because:

  > It is "from God"
  > Early Christians believed that it was inspired
  > The Bible is a diverse book, but unified in its message
  > The Holy Spirit confirms that it is inspired to our heart

- God still speaks to us through the Bible.

- We must obey what God tells us through His Word.

Practicing

Ask the group, "What can you do this week to improve your practice of Bible reading, study, and memorization?"

Encourage group members to use the Personal Spiritual Journal pages that accompany each chapter of the *Building Faith* books.

Closing

Consider bringing your session to a close by reading a Scripture in unison, such as Psalm 119:33–40.

Before you dismiss:

- Remind group members to pray for one another during the week.

- Say, "Next week, we'll have a fishing lesson—you'll learn some things about 'fishing for men,' that is, sharing the good news with others."

CHAPTER 4

Sharing the Good News with Others

Evangelism

Focus

This chapter is about sharing the Christian faith with other people. Sharing the faith is compared to fishing. Using the fishing analogy, you will discover practical ways to witness to nonbelievers.

Discovery: We fulfill Christ's Great Commission (Matt. 28:18–20) by "going fishing for people" (Matt. 4:19).

Preparing

❏ Read chapter 4 of *Knowing Christ: believing.*

❏ Review Matt. 4:19 and Matt. 28:19–20 and note your insights.

❏ Review the Observing section of this lesson to identify the concepts that you will lead your group to discover.

❏ Choose an activity from "Icebreakers."

❏ Choose a teaching method from "Leader's Toolbox" that will help your group arrive at the discovery for this session.

❏ Choose a learning activity from "Memory Verse Learning Methods."

❏ Gather the materials you'll need for this session.

❏ Ask the Holy Spirit to give you wisdom for communicating his truth.

Hint: Everyone can use a little encouragement. E-mail or call your group members during the week to tell them that you appreciate their participation in *Building Faith.*

Suggested Object Lesson: Fishing Pole

Ask, "When was the last time you went fishing? Let's find out what it means to be 'fishers of men.'"

Suggested Songs

"Fishers of Men" (Traditional); "I Love to Tell the Story" (A. Catherine Hankey); "Shine, Jesus, Shine" (Graham Kendrick).

Connecting

Use the icebreaker to encourage group members to share with one another. Then take a minute to encourage group members to talk about how they are applying the lessons of *Building Faith* to their personal lives. Allow time for responses. Review prayer concerns from the last session and invite the group to share new requests for prayer. Lead the group in praying together.

Hint: Encourage group members to connect with one another during the week. Relationship building can take place outside the group meetings! You might want to schedule a get together event before or after class.

Discovering

Review the important Scriptures for this session, giving special attention to those portions in italics. The key verse is printed in bold. Before you begin, ask, "What was the last thing Jesus said to His disciples?"

Matthew 28:18–20

[18]Then Jesus came to them and said, "All authority in heaven and on earth has been given to me. [19]Therefore *go and make disciples* of all nations, *baptizing* them in the name of the Father, and of the Son and of the Holy Spirit [20]and *teaching* them *to obey* everything I have commanded you. And surely, *I will be with you* always, to the very end of the age."

Matthew 4:19

"*Come, follow me*," Jesus said, "and *I will make you fishers* of men."

Use these questions to the group connect God's Word to life. Suggest that they write their responses:

- According to these verses, what are the tasks that Jesus gave us?

- If you were to use a modern analogy for making disciples (instead of "fishing for men") what would it be? Why?

- How well do you think Christians are doing at making disciples these days?

Memorizing

Lead your group in memorizing Matt. 4:19, using one of the activities from "Memory Verse Learning Methods." Remind your group that before printed Bibles were common, all Christians relied on Scripture memorization to learn God's Word, and persecuted Christians still do!

Observing

The key points to observe in this session are:

- Christians are called to make disciples.

- There are various approaches to evangelism based on the personal style of the evangelist.

- To make disciples, we must get into contact with nonbelievers.

- To make disciples, we must present the gospel and call for a decision.

- Conversion is the beginning, not the end, of the process of disciple making.

Practicing

Encourage the members of your group to set a "fishing appointment" within the next two weeks. Ask them to review their top ten list from session two and circle the name of the person with whom they will aim to share the good news.

Closing

Bring session to a close by offering a prayer, singing a song, or offering an affirmation and blessing.

Before you dismiss:

- Remind group members to use the Scripture memory flash cards that are included in *Knowing Christ: believing.*

- Ask, "Do you think it's possible to become the person you really want to be? We'll find out next week!"

CHAPTER 5

Growing Deeper in the Christian Life

Holiness

Focus

This session reveals that God wants to change your heart so that you can live the good life you've always wanted to live. That process will begin when you offer your whole life as a sacrifice to Him.

Discovery: God can make you the person you really want to be.

Preparing

❏ Read chapter 5 of *Knowing Christ: believing.*

❏ Review 1 Thess. 4:3 and 1 Thess. 5:23–24 and note your insights.

❏ Review the Observing section of this lesson to identify the concepts that you will lead your group to discover.

❏ Choose an activity from "Icebreakers."

❏ Choose a teaching method from "Leader's Toolbox" that will help your group arrive at the discovery for this session.

❏ Choose a learning activity from "Memory Verse Learning Methods."

❏ Gather the materials you'll need for this session.

❏ Review the chart "Sin and Sanctification" on page 105 of *Knowing Christ: believing,* which addresses many questions that people have about holiness.

❏ Plan a response time for the conclusion of this lesson. Include an invitation for students to take the "next step" in surrendering their lives to God.

❏ Gather the materials you'll need for this session. There are three

special brochures on this topic: "FAQs about Life in the Spirit,"
"Terms & Truths about Holiness," and "Filled to the Brim." These
are available through Wesleyan Publishing House.

❏ Pray that God will use this important lesson to move someone
close to Him.

Hint: Personal testimony is an incredibly powerful teaching tool.
Think about your own experience of sanctification and be prepared to talk
about how you have approached the issue of consecration and have
experienced the Holy Spirit's work.

Suggested Object Lesson: Laundry Soap

Read some of the statement manufacturer's statements (from the box)
about how to get clothes clean. Say, "Today we will discover how to
become spiritually pure."

Suggested Songs

"Create in Me a Clean Heart" (Unknown); "Holy Spirit, Rain Down"
(Russell Fragar); "Called Unto Holiness" (Leila Naylor Morris); "Breathe
on Me, Breath of God" (Edwin Hatch).

Connecting

Use the icebreaker to encourage group members to share with one
another. Then take a minute to encourage group members to talk about
how they are applying the lessons of *Building Faith* to their personal
lives. Allow time for responses. Review prayer concerns from the last
session and invite the group to share new requests for prayer. Lead the
group in praying together.

Hint: The icebreaker can be a great way to introduce the subject of
the session. Consider using an icebreaker that incorporates the theme of
this chapter.

Discovering

Review the important Scriptures for this session, giving special attention
to those portions in italics. The key verse is printed in bold. Before you
begin, ask , "Do you think it's possible for human nature to be changed?"

1 Thessalonians 5:23–24

> [23]May God himself, the God of peace, sanctify you through and through. May your whole spirit, soul and body be kept blameless at the coming of our Lord Jesus Christ. [24]The one who calls you is faithful and he will do it.

1 Thessalonians 4:3

> *It is God's will that you should be sanctified. . . .*

Use these questions to the group connect God's Word to life. Suggest that they write their responses:

- What do these Scriptures tell you about God's will?

- What does sanctify mean?

- What do you think it means to keep blameless? How would you go about keeping your spirit, soul, and body blameless?

Memorizing

Lead your group in memorizing 1 Thess. 4:3, using one of the activities from "Memory Verse Learning Methods." Encourage the group to review the memory verses between sessions by using the flash cards printed at the end of *Knowing Christ: believing.*

Observing

The key points to observe in this session are:

- It is God's will for us to be holy.

- God did not command us to be holy in order to frustrate us. He really means to change us!

- Sanctification has two meanings: consecration and purification.

- When we consecrate our lives to God, He changes us.

Practicing

Review the example of the houseguest on page 99 of *Knowing Christ: believing.* Lead your group to a moment of consecration. Ask:

- Have you ever consecrated your life to God?

- Have you discovered some rooms of your house that are closed to Him?

- Are you ready to dedicate your entire life to His service?

Closing

Close your time together by inviting group members to consecrate their lives to God and leading them in a prayer of consecration.

Before you dismiss:

- Encourage group members to make use of the Personal Spiritual Journal pages included in each chapter of *Knowing Christ: believing*

- Say, "Next week, we'll find out why *worship* is a verb."

CHAPTER 6

Learning to Put God First

Worship

Focus

In this session, you will learn what worship is, why it is important for Christians, and some ways that it may be done. You'll review the history of worship and its theological foundations, and you'll discover why both public (corporate) and private (individual) worship are important.

Discovery: Worship is something that you *do*.

Preparing

❏ Read chapter 6 of *Knowing Christ: believing.*

❏ Review Ps. 150:1–6 and note your insights.

❏ Review the Observing section of this lesson to identify the concepts that you will lead your group to discover.

❏ Choose an activity from "Icebreakers."

❏ Choose a teaching method from "Leader's Toolbox" that will help your group arrive at the discovery for this session.

❏ Choose a learning activity from "Memory Verse Learning Methods."

❏ Prepare a sheet for each attendee that has the Lord's Prayer written on it (to be used at the end of this session).

❏ Gather the materials you'll need for this session. Consider using a whiteboard or flip chart to write down group members' responses.

❏ Pray for each member of your group by name.

Hint: Some group members enjoy doing small learning assignments. Consider enlisting a group member to interview three friends on the meaning of *worship* and share his or her findings as an introduction to this session.

Suggested Object Lesson: Hymn book, communion cup, water.

Ask, "What do these items have in common?" They are all used in worship. Say, "Today, we'll learn why it is so important for believers to spend time in worship."

Suggested Songs

"All Hail the Power of Jesus' Name" (Edward Perronet); "Majesty" (Jack Hayford); "I Worship You, Almighty God" (Sondra Corbett).

Connecting

Use the icebreaker to encourage group members to share with one another. Then take a minute to encourage group members to talk about how they are applying the lessons of *Building Faith* to their personal lives. Allow time for responses. You may want to spend some of this time in worship. Review prayer concerns from the last session and invite the group to share new requests for prayer. Lead the group in praying together.

Hint: People love to be called by name. Greet each person by name as he or she arrives.

Discovering

Review the important Scriptures for this session, giving special attention to those portions in italics. The key verse is printed in bold. Before you begin, ask them to circle (or point out) the words that suggest *variety* and *intensity* during worship.

Psalm 150:1–6

¹*Praise the Lord.* Praise God in his *sanctuary*; praise him in his *mighty heavens.* ²Praise him for *his acts of power*; praise him for *his surpassing greatness.* ³Praise him with the *sounding of the trumpet*, praise him with *the harp and lyre*, ⁴praise him with *the tambourine and dancing*, praise him with the *strings and flute*, ⁵praise him with the *clash of symbols*, praise him with resounding cymbals. ⁶**Let everything that has breath praise the Lord. Praise the Lord.**

Ask students to write down their answers to these questions, then share their responses with the group.

- What methods of worship are included in this passage?

- What does this Psalm tell you about how you should worship God?

- How do people's preferences affect the way they worship?

Memorizing

Lead your group in memorizing Psalm 150:6, using one of the activities from "Memory Verse Learning Methods." Consider offering a gift (perhaps a copy of *The Message* or some other translation of the Bible) to anyone who memorizes all of the key verses. You may want to remind them of the memory verse cards at the end of their books.

Observing

The key points to observe in this session are:

- It is important for God's people to worship corporately (together).

- Worship styles may vary in intensity and activity.

- The five purposes of worship are ascribe, align, acknowledge, admit, and admire (see pages 117–118 of *Knowing Christ: believing*).

- Worship is a verb as well as a noun (it is something we must *do*).

Practicing

Review the two approaches to personal worship found on page 114 of *Knowing Christ: believing*. Challenge your group members to spend fifteen minutes each day in worship and recording their experiences to share next week.

Closing

Bring this session to a close by praying the Lord's Prayer together. Before you dismiss:

- Encourage your group members to maintain a daily time of prayer and Bible reading.

- Ask, "Does your life seem a little bit chaotic? Next week, we'll find out how to order our lives around God's priorities."

CHAPTER 7

Managing Your Life with God in Mind

Stewardship

Focus

God has charged us with the responsibility of being stewards of everything in our lives. We are commanded to love the Lord our God with all our heart, soul, mind, and strength and our neighbor as ourselves. This session explores the impact this command on our attitude toward possessions, family, and God.

Discovery: Life works best when we place all of our resources—as well as all we are—under God's control.

Preparing

❏ Read chapter 7 of *Knowing Christ: believing*.

❏ Review Jer. 1:5; 1 Cor. 6:19–20; Ezek. 18:4; and Mark 12:30–31 and note your insights.

❏ Review the Observing section of this lesson to identify the concepts that you will lead your group to discover.

❏ Choose an activity from "Icebreakers."

❏ Choose a teaching method from "Leader's Toolbox" that will help your group arrive at the discovery for this session. Since there are many biblical references to stewardship, consider brining a Bible concordance to your meeting so group members can do a mini study on *stewardship, tithe,* or *wealth.*

❏ Choose a learning activity from "Memory Verse Learning Methods."

❏ Gather the materials you'll need for this session.

❏ Pray about the prayer requests that have been mentioned recently in your group.

Hint: Current events make great attention getters. You may wish to gather recent news stories that deal with personal or public finances as a starter for this session.

Suggested Object Lesson: A Watch or Clock

Say, "Time is one of the things we must manage wisely. Talent and treasure are others. Let's find out how."

Suggested Songs

"Give of Your Best to the Master" (Howard B. Grose); "More Precious than Silver" (Lynn DeShazo); "In My Life, Lord, Be Glorified" (Bob Kilpatrick).

Connecting

Use the icebreaker to encourage group members to share with one another. Then take a minute to encourage group members to talk about how they are applying the lessons of *Building Faith* to their personal lives. Allow time for responses. Review prayer concerns from the last session and invite the group to share new requests for prayer. Lead the group in praying together.

Hint: People who are unwilling to pray in a large group may be willing to pray in a group of two or three.

Discovering

Review the important Scriptures for this session, giving special attention to those portions in italics. The key verse is printed in bold. Before you begin, ask your group, "What does it mean to love someone?"

Jeremiah 1:5

Before I formed you in the womb *I knew you, before you were born* I set you apart. . . .

1 Corinthians 6:19–20

[19]Do you not know that *your body is a temple of the Holy Spirit*, who is in you, whom you have received from God? You are not your own; [20]*you were bought* at a price. Therefore honor God with your body.

Ezekiel 18:4

For *every living soul belongs to me*, the father as well as the son—both alike belong to me.

Mark 12:30–31

[30]*Love the Lord* your God with all your *heart* and with all your *soul* and with all your *mind* and with all your *strength.* [31]The second is this: *love your neighbor as yourself.* There is no commandment greater than these.

Ask your group:

- What does it mean to love the Lord with all your heart, soul, mind, and strength?

- How do you show your love for God in the way you live?

Memorizing

Lead your group in memorizing Mark 12:30–31, using one of the activities from "Memory Verse Learning Methods." Encourage the group to review the memory verses between sessions by using the flash cards printed at the end of *Knowing Christ: believing.* If you have chosen this option, remind them that you will present a gift to each person who memorizes all of the key verses for this study series.

Observing

The key points to observe in this session are:

- Managing our lives well begins with loving God wholeheartedly.

- Managing our lives well involves loving others.

- Everything that we have belongs to God; we manage it for Him.

- Managing our lives well means loving and providing for our families.

Practicing

Ask group members to silently review the items that they've spent money on in the past week. Ask, "If our debit card receipts reveal our priorities, what do your spending habits say about you?" Challenge members to identify one area of spending that should come under tighter control.

Closing

To close your session, ask a group member to pray that Jesus will be established as Lord in each member's life.

Before you dismiss:

- Remind group members to keep in touch during the week by phone or E-mail, and to pray for one another.

- Say, "Next week we'll find out why there is no such thing as a Lone-Ranger Christian."

CHAPTER 8

Becoming Part of the Family

Fellowship

Focus

John Wesley observed that "there is no such thing as a solitary Christian." We really do need each other. This session helps believers see that the Christian life can't be lived in isolation. You'll learn why fellowship, the sacraments, and becoming part of a local church are important for the Christian life.

Discovery: Christians need the encouragement and support of one another.

Preparing

❏ Read chapter 8 of *Knowing Christ: believing.*

❏ Review Eph. 2:2–6, 11–16; Matt. 4:19; and Matt. 28:19–20, noting your insights.

❏ Review the Observing section of this lesson to identify the concepts that you will lead your group to discover.

❏ Choose an activity from "Icebreakers."

❏ Choose a teaching method from "Leader's Toolbox" that will help your group arrive at the discovery for this session.

❏ Choose a learning activity from "Memory Verse Learning Methods."

❏ Gather the materials you'll need for this session.

❏ Prepare gifts for those who have memorized all key verses, if this is something that you have planned to do.

❏ Pray for your group as they continue to grow in the faith.

Hint: Experience is a powerful learning tool. If circumstances permit, speak with your pastor about having the group attend a baptism or receive the Lord's Supper together as part of this session.

Suggested Object Lesson: Family Photo

Ask, "How many people are in your family? Today we'll learn about your other family—the family of God."

Suggested Songs

"Blest Be the Tie that Binds" (John Fawcett); "The Family of God" (William Gaither); "Leaning on the Everlasting Arms" (Elisha A. Hoffman); "Bind Us Together" (Bob Gillman).

Connecting

Use the icebreaker to encourage group members to share with one another. Then take a minute to encourage group members to talk about how they are applying the lessons of *Building Faith* to their personal lives. Allow time for responses. Review prayer concerns from the last session and invite the group to share new requests for prayer. Lead the group in praying together.

Hint: Use the Connecting time to help the group reflect on how they have grown by being part of this group. Ask, "What has the Lord taught you over the past several weeks?"

Discovering

Review the important Scriptures for this session, giving special attention to those portions in italics. The key verse is printed in bold. Before you begin, ask, "Name something that is impossible to do alone." Point out that being a Christian is a team sport, since we depend on the fellowship of one another.

Ephesians 4:2-6, 11-16

²Be completely *humble and gentle*; be patient, *bearing with one another in love.* ³Make every effort to *keep the unity* of the Spirit through the bond of peace. ⁴There is one body and one Spirit—just as you were *called to one hope* when you were called— ⁵one Lord, one faith, one baptism; ⁶one God and Father of all, who is over all and through all and in all. . . . ¹¹It was he who gave some to be

apostles, some to be *prophets*, some to be *evangelists*, and some to be *pastors and teachers*, [12]to prepare God's people for the *works of service*, so that the body of Christ may be built up [13]until we all reach *unity in the faith* and in the knowledge of the Son of God and *become mature*, attaining to the whole measure of the *fullness of Christ*. [14]Then we will no longer be infants, tossed back and forth by the waves, and blown here and there by every wind of teaching and by the cunning and craftiness of men in their deceitful scheming. [15]Instead, *speaking the truth in love*, we will in all things *grow up* into him who is the Head, that is Christ. [16]**From him *the whole body*, joined and held together by every supporting ligament, *grows and builds itself up in love*, as each part does its work.**

Ask group members to share answers to these questions:

- What do these Scriptures tell you about the Church?

- In what ways do these verses confirm or conflict with your ideas about the Church?

- What role might you have in the body of Christ? What are you doing to fulfill it?

Memorizing

Lead your group in memorizing Eph. 4:16, using one of the activities from "Memory Verse Learning Methods." Remind the group to continue the habit of Scripture memorization even after this study has concluded. If you have chosen to do so, give gifts to those who have memorized all of the key verses for this study.

Observing

The key points to observe in this session are:

- The Christian life is not a life of isolation but a life of fellowship in the Body of Christ.

- Baptism, communion, local church involvement, and accountability all require interaction with people and cannot be done in isolation.

- Christians need each other for fellowship, encouragement, and assistance.

- The church is not perfect, but it is God's plan to impact the world.

Practicing

Ask your group members whether or not they have been baptized. Encourage those who have not to consider baptism.

If all members of your group have been baptized, challenge them to consider becoming a member of the local church.

Closing

Bring your session to a close by offering a prayer, asking that God will continue to lead each group member to grow in the faith.

Before you dismiss:

- Invite group members to continue their spiritual journey by joining a Sunday School class or small group.

- Encourage group members to continue learning with the next volume in the *Building Faith* series, *Growing in Christ: becoming*.

Growing in Christ

becoming

Session Plans

Growing in Christ

Leader's Introduction

All living things grow: plants, trees, animals, people, and yes, even faith in Christ. Every believer's faith must be growing continually. Growth and development are essential for spiritual health. The opposite of growth is decay, which leads to death. That is not a pleasant prospect, but it can become a reality for anyone who doesn't take spiritual growth seriously.

Spiritual growth is important—and not just to you, but also for your students. Pastors, Sunday School teachers or small group leaders, Christian relatives and friends along with you are all vitally interested in seeing your students reach spiritual maturity. In fact, your Heavenly Father takes a direct interest in their spiritual condition! Growing as a believer was not meant to be a solo adventure. It's a journey we take together, a journey called *discipleship.*

And that's where the *Building Faith* series comes in. It is a series of books that will help your students grow in the faith, and in the book, *Growing in Christ: becoming,* is a vital part of that plan for growth.

As your students open the pages of this book, they'll gain the insight they need to become more and more like Christ. The goal is that they will become all that God wants them to be—a living representation of Jesus Christ. That won't happen in a day, a week, or even a year, but they will get there. It's a lifelong journey, and they'll make progress every day.

This book is designed to be your personal guide on the discipleship journey.

Many great discoveries await your group members! Here are a few of the milestones they'll pass as they explore *Growing in Christ: becoming.*

Chapter one will help them scan the horizon from a new perspective. It's about developing a Christian worldview—it will help them form a uniquely Christian way of looking at life.

Using our resources for God's glory is the focus of chapter two. There they'll discover that faithful use of all God has entrusted to us is part of His plan for our growth.

Discipline. Few of us like that word, but we all need it. Chapter three will explore the how and why of spiritual disciplines—those practices and habits that help us become more like Christ.

The fourth chapter delves into one of the greatest mysteries in Scripture—the Trinity. They will gain a greater understanding of our awesome God and come away inspired to worship.

The snapshot of Christian history in chapter five will whet their appetite for the study of our rich heritage. They'll meet some of the reformers and revivalists who have shaped the church over the centuries.

What we believe really does make a difference in the way we live. They'll see that in chapter six as they discover the core biblical teachings about faith and salvation.

The final chapter will introduce them to two foundational Scriptures—the Ten Commandments and the Sermon on the Mount. There they'll begin to learn how to study the Bible for themselves.

There's a lot to learn, so let's get started on the exciting journey of *Building Faith!*

RAY E. BARNWELL, SR.

Learning to Think Like a Christian

Worldview

Focus

This session forces believers to examine the way they think about God, themselves, and the world around them. You'll discover that Christians think differently than nonbelievers because they see the world in a different way. That unique perspective is based on biblical values.

Discovery: Our understanding of God's Word shapes the way we think about everything else.

Preparing

❏ Read chapter 1 of *Growing in Christ: becoming.*

❏ Review Eph. 1:17–23 and Gal. 2:20 and note your personal insights.

❏ Review the Observing section of this lesson to identify the concepts that you will lead your group to discover.

❏ Choose an activity from "Icebreakers."

❏ Choose a teaching method from "Leader's Toolbox" that will help your group arrive at the discovery for this session.

❏ Choose a learning activity from "Memory Verse Learning Methods."

❏ To illustrate the concept of *worldview* to your group, be prepared to give your own definition and show one example of how your worldview has shaped a decision you've made.

❏ Gather the materials you'll need for this session.

❏ Pray that God will use this study to transform lives.

Hint: Remember to vary your teaching methods from week to week. You can also use more than one method in a single session.

Suggested Object Lesson: A Globe

Pass the globe around so that each person holds it in his or her hands, then move the globe to the end of the room. Ask the group to thing about viewing the world from God's perspective. Say, "Today we will discover how to develop a Christian worldview."

Suggested Songs

"Be Thou My Vision" (Traditional Irish Hymn); "He's Got the Whole World in His Hands" (Traditional); "Shine, Jesus, Shine" (Graham Kendrick).

Connecting

Greet each member of your group and welcome off of them to the *Building Faith* series. Explain that the purpose of these sessions is to *help believers grow* in their new life in Christ.

People need to warm up to each other before they'll share the important things in their lives, so use one or more icebreaker activities to encourage relationship building.

If this group is a group that has met before and has already established relationships, continue the sharing, caring, and prayer time, using a variety of approaches.

If this is a new group, tell them that *prayer, caring, and sharing* each other's concerns will be an important part of what you do together. Invite group members to share:

- Praise Items—Good things that God has done in their lives lately

- Prayer Requests—Concerns for themselves or for a friend

- Needs—Things in their lives or in the community that the group might be able to help with

Consider enlisting someone to record prayer requests and praise items for the group each week—that will help you remember to pray consistently for important needs and celebrate answers to prayer.

Lead the group in a time of prayer. Remember, there are lots of ways for a group to pray together. See the "Leader's Toolbox" for some ideas.

Discovering

Review the important Scriptures for this session, giving special attention to those portions in italics. The key verse is printed in bold. Before you begin, ask, "What is the hardest thing about living and working alongside people who are not Christians?" Point out that Christians tend to see the world differently because of their faith.

Ephesians 1:17–23

[17]I keep asking that the God of our Lord Jesus Christ, the glorious Father, may *give you the Spirit of wisdom and revelation*, so that you may know him better. [18]I pray also that the eyes of your *heart may be enlightened* in order that you may *know the hope* to which he has called you, *the riches of his glorious inheritance* in the saints, [19]and *his incomparably great power for us* who believe. That power is like the working of his mighty strength, [20]which he exerted in Christ when he raised him from the dead and seated him at his right hand in the heavenly realms [21]far *above all rule and authority*, *power and dominion*, and *every title* that can be given, not only in the present age but also in the one to come. [22]And *God placed all things under his feet* and appointed him to be head over everything, for the *church,* [23]*which is his body*, the fullness of him who fills everything in every way.

Galatians 2:20

I have been crucified with Christ and *I no longer live*, but *Christ lives in me*. The life I live in the body, *I live by faith in the Son of God*, who loved me and gave himself for me.

Ask group members to share their responses to these questions:

- How are we to view our life, the world around us, and our purpose here?

- In what ways do these verses help you develop a Christian worldview?

Point out that when Christ is the Lord of our lives, our priorities must be reordered.

Memorizing

Lead your group in memorizing Gal. 2:20, using one of the activities from "Memory Verse Learning Methods." Encourage the group to review the memory verses between sessions by using the flash cards printed at the end of *Growing in Christ: becoming.* You may also want to encourage them to memorize by offering a gift to everyone who memorizes all the verses.

Observing

The key points to observe in this session are:

- Worldview is a comprehensive way of looking at life that shapes our decision making and interaction with others.

- Family, culture, peers, education, and faith influence worldview.

- Contemporary culture has a tremendous influence on the worldview of our children.

- A Christian worldview produces hope and freedom.

Practicing

Challenge group members to apply a biblical worldview to their decision making. Ask, "What's the most important issue that you're facing right now? What does the Bible say that influences your reaction or decision about this matter?" Allow group members to respond aloud.

Closing

Bring your session to a close by offering a prayer, singing a song, or offering an affirmation and blessing.

Before you dismiss:

- Remind group members to bring a Bible to each session.

- Encourage group members to continue their spiritual journey by joining a Sunday School class or small group.

- Say, "Next week, we'll find out how to make the most of what God has given to us."

CHAPTER 2

Living on Borrowed Time

Stewardship

Focus

This session helps believers apply the lordship of Christ to the practical areas of time, talent, and treasure. It's important for all Christians to manage their lives well. When we do that, we can have a tremendous impact on our church and community.

Discovery: Everything that we have belongs to God.

Preparing

❏ Read chapter 2 of *Growing in Christ: becoming.*

❏ Review Matt. 25:14–30 and note your insights.

❏ Review the Observing section of this lesson to identify the concepts that you will lead your group to discover.

❏ Choose an activity from "Icebreakers."

❏ Choose a teaching method from "Leader's Toolbox" that will help your group arrive at the discovery for this session.

❏ Choose a learning activity from "Memory Verse Learning Methods." Consider using the exercise on page 48 of *Growing in Christ: becoming* with your group.

❏ Gather the materials you'll need for this session. You may want to use a spiritual gifts inventory for the Practicing section of this lesson.

❏ Pray for each member of your group by name.

Hint: Some group members may be more comfortable writing their reactions than speaking aloud in class.

Suggested Object Lesson: Ball Cap with "BOSS" Written on It

Ask, "Who is in charge of your life?"

Suggested Songs

"Seek Ye First" (Karen Lafferty); "Give of Your Best to the Master" (Howard B. Grose); "My Life Is in You, Lord" (Daniel Gardner); "All For Jesus, All For Jesus" (Mary D. James).

Connecting

Use an icebreaker activity to encourage relationship building.

As a follow-up of the discussion on spiritual formation, you might invite group members to share one decision they made recently that was affected by their view of the world.

Invite group members to share:

- Praise Items—Good things that God has done in their lives lately

- Prayer Requests—Concerns for themselves or for a friend

- Needs—Things in their lives or in the community that the group might be able to help with

Review prayer requests from the last session, and lead the group in a time of prayer. Remember, there are lots of ways for a group to pray together. See the "Leader's Toolbox" for some ideas.

Discovering

The story Jesus told in Matt. 25:14–30 illustrates the importance of faithful management of our resources. Review the important Scriptures for this session, giving special attention to those portions in italics. The key verse is printed in bold.

Before you begin, ask, "Is there anything you own that you could not live without?" Observe that the things we own often come to own us!

Matthew 25:14–30

[14]"Again, it will be like a man going on a journey, who called his servants and *entrusted his property to them.* [15]To one he gave five talents of money, to another two talents, and to another one talent, each *according to his ability.* Then he went on his journey. [16]The man who

had received the five talents went at once and *put his money to work and gained five more.* [17]So also, the one with the two talents gained two more. [18]But the man who had received the one talent went off, *dug a hole in the ground and hid his master's money.* [19]After a long time the master of those servants *returned and settled accounts* with them. [20]The man who had received the five talents brought the other five. "Master," he said, "you entrusted me with five talents. See, I have gained five more." [21]**His master replied, "*Well done, good and faithful servant! You have been faithful with a few things; I will put you in charge of many things.* Come and share your master's happiness!"** [22]"The man with the two talents also came. "Master," he said, "you entrusted me with two talents; see, I have gained two more." [23]His master replied, "*Well done, good and faithful servant! You have been faithful with a few things; I will put you in charge of many things.* Come and share your master's happiness!" [24]Then the man who had received the one talent came. "Master," he said, "I knew that you are a hard man, harvesting where you have not sown and gathering where you have not scattered seed. [25]So *I was afraid and went out and hid your talent* in the ground. See, here is what belongs to you." [26]His master replied, "You wicked, lazy servant! So you knew that I harvest where I have not sown and gather where I have not scattered seed? [27]Well then, *you should have put my money on deposit* with the bankers, so that when I returned *I would have received it back with interest.* [28]Take the talent from him and give it to the one who has the ten talents. [29]For *everyone who has will be given more*, and he will have an abundance. Whoever does not have, even what he has will be taken from him. [30]And throw that worthless servant outside, into the darkness, where there will be weeping and gnashing of teeth."

Have the group members work in teams of two to review these passages. Ask them to answer the following questions together.

- Review the details of the story: number of servants, what each was given, and what they did with it.

- What are the key words or ideas in Matt. 25:14–30?

- How can this parable apply to you today?

Especially emphasize that all of us, as Christ's disciples, are given responsibilities based on our abilities. We then choose what we will do with them.

Memorizing

Lead your group in memorizing Matt. 25:21, using one of the activities from "Memory Verse Learning Methods." Remind your group that memorized Scripture is a Bible that can be taken anywhere.

Observing

The key points to observe in this session are:

- Stewardship means managing our talents, treasures, and time with God in mind.

- Stewardship has the practical value of enhancing our churches and communities.

- We are called by God to be good stewards of what He has given to us.

Practicing

Challenge the members of your group to take a spiritual gifts inventory, if they have not done so, to become aware of what their spiritual gifts are. You may also wish to duplicate the Response Card from the "Resources" chapter of this book and use it to encourage group members to commit themselves to the practice of tithing.

Closing

Bring this session to a close by thanking God for the resources He has given us, then praying for the wisdom and discipline to use your time, talent, and treasure effectively.

Before you dismiss:

- Encourage group members to make use of the Personal Spiritual Journal pages included in each chapter of *Growing in Christ: becoming.*

- Ask, "How do you keep yourself spiritually fit? We'll find out next week."

CHAPTER 3

Habits of a Healthy Heart

Spiritual Disciplines

Focus

The spiritual disciplines of prayer, meditation, fasting, Bible study, and memorization can lead to a holy life. This session challenges believers to develop good habits that will keep their spiritual life in tune.

Discovery: Spiritual disciplines bring spiritual power.

Preparing

❏ Read chapter 3 of *Growing in Christ: becoming.*

❏ Review Col. 3:1–17 and note your insights on spiritual discipline and the holy life.

❏ Review the Observing section of this lesson to identify the concepts that you will lead your group to discover.

❏ Choose an activity from "Icebreakers."

❏ Choose a teaching method from "Leader's Toolbox" that will help your group arrive at the discovery for this session.

❏ Choose a learning activity from "Memory Verse Learning Methods."

❏ Gather the materials you'll need for this session. Make copies of the charts The Holy Life, Components of Prayer, and Bible Study Loop, which are found in the "Resources" section of this book and on page 63 of *Growing in Christ: becoming.*

❏ Pray for your spiritual growth as you lead others in *Building Faith.*

Hint: Many people are visual learners. Consider using a prop or visual aid in this session.

Suggested Object Lesson: Diet Book

Ask, "Have you ever been on a diet? How did it go? Today we'll talk about having a healthy spiritual diet."

Suggested Songs

"Take Time to Be Holy" (William D. Longstaff); "What a Friend We Have in Jesus" (Joseph M. Scriven); "Step by Step" (Beaker); "Near to the Heart of God" (Cleland B. McAfee).

Connecting

Use the icebreaker to encourage group members to share with one another. Then take a minute to encourage group members to talk about how they are applying the lessons of *Building Faith* to their personal lives. Allow time for responses. Review prayer concerns from the last session and invite the group to share new requests for prayer. Lead the group in praying together.

Hint: Remember that group interaction begins prior to the session itself. That's why room arrangement is important and a circle arrangement often best.

Discovering

Review the important Scriptures for this session, giving special attention to those portions in italics. The key verse is printed in bold. Before you begin, ask, "If you exercise to keep your body healthy, what can you do to keep your spirit healthy?"

Colossians 3:12–17

[12]Therefore as God's chosen people, holy and dearly loved, clothe yourselves with *compassion, kindness, humility, gentleness and patience.* [13]*Bear with each* other and *forgive whatever grievances you may have against one another.* Forgive as the Lord forgave you. [14]And over all these virtues *put on love,* which binds them all together in perfect unity. [15]*Let the peace of Christ rule in your hearts,* since as members of one body you were called to peace. And *be thankful.* [16]Let the word of Christ dwell in you richly as you *teach and admonish one another* with all wisdom, and as you *sing psalms, hymns and spiritual*

songs with gratitude in your hearts to God. [17]**And *whatever you do*, whether in word or deed, *do it all in the name of the Lord Jesus*, giving thanks to God the Father through him.**

Ask students to write their answers to these questions:

- How can you clothe yourself with compassion, kindness, humility, gentleness, and patience?

- Why is love the virtue to put on over all others?

- How are we to live according to this passage?

Memorizing

Lead your group in memorizing Gal. 3:17, using one of the activities from "Memory Verse Learning Methods." Remind group members that memorizing God's Word builds their strength to resist temptation and helps them make choices that please God.

Observing

The key points to observe in this session are:

- Spiritual disciplines help to build a holy life.

- Prayer is communication with God, and there are various ways to pray.

- Meditation is focused thinking in the presence of God, which leads to greater understanding and helps to build a holy life.

- Fasting is voluntary abstinence, which places spiritual growth above physical appetites.

- Bible study and memorization lead to life transformation.

- Spiritual disciplines are our weapons for fighting temptation.

Practicing

Challenge your group members to adopt one new spiritual discipline. Members who do not now practice any of the disciplines noted in this session should be encouraged to begin with a daily time of prayer. Remind the group members there are pages for journal writing at the end of each chapter and book.

Closing

Bring your session to a close by praying for each person by name. Ask that God will help them to develop spiritual disciplines.

Before you dismiss:

- Remind group members to pray for one another during the week.

- Say, "Next week, you will learn how to explain the fact that God is both one and three and the same time—and why it matters!"

CHAPTER 4

The Mystery of God

The Trinity

Focus

This session explores the distinctly Christian doctrine of the Trinity. You will understand the concept that God is Three-in-One by examining Scriptures and reviewing what the early church believed about God. You'll also discover how this concept affects how you know and worship God.

Discovery: There is one God, who exists in three distinct Persons.

Preparing

- ❏ Read chapter 4 of *Growing in Christ: becoming.*

- ❏ Review Matt. 3:13–17, 28:18–20; and 2 Cor. 13:14 and note the ways that each informs our understanding of the Trinity.

- ❏ Review the Observing section of this lesson to identify the concepts that you will lead your group to discover.

- ❏ Choose an activity from "Icebreakers."

- ❏ Choose a teaching method from "Leader's Toolbox" that will help your group arrive at the discovery for this session.

- ❏ Choose a learning activity from "Memory Verse Learning Methods."

- ❏ Ask the Holy Spirit to give you wisdom for communicating His truth.

- ❏ Gather the materials you'll need for this session. Consider using the chart Compare These Passages, found in the "Resources" section of this book, to review the concept of "three-in-one" with your group.

- ❏ Note in the "Resources" section of this book the graphic of three interlaced rings representing the inseparable Threeness-in-Oneness of the Father, Son and Holy Spirit. Note how each ring passes through the other two—symbolizing that nothing one "person" is or does is ever separate from the other two.

Hint: Everyone can use a little encouragement. E-mail or call your group members during the week to tell them that you appreciate their participation in *Building Faith.*

Suggested Object Lesson: An Apple

Cut the apple in half to show that it consists of three distinct parts: the skin, the meat, and the core. These three parts together make one apple. Say, "In the same way, God is three in one. Today, we'll see why that's true—and why it is important."

Suggested Songs

"Holy, Holy, Holy" (Reginald Heber); "Father, I Adore You" (Terrye Coelho); "There Is a Redeemer" (Melody Green); "Come, Thou Almighty King" (Anonymous).

Connecting

Use the icebreaker to encourage group members to share with one another. Then take a minute to encourage group members to talk about how they are applying the lessons of *Building Faith* to their personal lives. Allow time for responses. Review prayer concerns from the last session and invite the group to share new requests for prayer. Lead the group in praying together.

Hint: Encourage group members to connect with one another during the week. Maybe you'll want to suggest having a meal or coffee together. Relationship building can take place outside the group meetings!

Discovering

Review the important Scriptures for this session, giving special attention to those portions in italics. The key verse is printed in bold. Before you begin, ask, "Does everything about the Bible have to make sense?" Point out that because God's mind is much greater than ours, there are some things about Him that are hard to understand.

Matthew 3:13–17

¹³Then Jesus came from Galilee to the Jordan to be baptized by John. ¹⁴But John tried to deter him, saying, "I need to be baptized by you, and do you come to me?" ¹⁵Jesus replied, "Let it be so now; it is proper for us to do this to fulfill all righteousness." Then John consented. ¹⁶As soon as *Jesus was baptized*, He went up out of the water. At that moment heaven was opened, and He saw the *Spirit of God descending like a dove* and lighting on him. ¹⁷And a *voice from heaven* said, "This is *my Son*, whom I love; with him I am well pleased."

Matthew 28:18–20

¹⁸Then Jesus came to them and said, "All authority in heaven and on earth has been given to me. ¹⁹**Therefore go and make disciples of all nations, baptizing them in the name of the *Father and of the Son and of the Holy Spirit*,** ²⁰and teaching them to obey everything I have commanded you. And surely *I am with you always*, to the very end of the age."

2 Corinthians 13:14

May the grace of the *Lord Jesus Christ*, and the love of *God*, and the fellowship of the *Holy Spirit* be with you all.

Ask group members to respond to these questions:

- What do these Scriptures tell you about God, Jesus, and the Holy Spirit?

- In what ways do these verses confirm or conflict with your ideas about who God is?

Especially emphasize that although there are three persons in the Trinity, He is one God.

Memorizing

Lead your group in memorizing Matt. 28:19, using one of the activities from "Memory Verse Learning Methods." Remind your group that before printed Bibles were common, all Christians relied on Scripture memorization to learn God's Word, and persecuted Christians still do!

Observing

The key points to observe in this session are:

- The New Testament conveys the idea that God is Three-in-One (the Trinity).

- The Old Testament also conveys the idea of the Trinity.

- The early church established the doctrine of the Trinity.

- The doctrine of the Trinity is beyond human understanding, though we can accept the reality of it by faith.

Practicing

Ask group members to reflect on how they interact with God as Father, Son, and Holy Spirit over the next week and record their insights to share.

Closing

Close your session by singing a song that emphasizes the Trinity, like the *Doxology; Glorify Thy Name; Holy, Holy, Holy! Lord God Almighty;* or *Holy, Holy.* Close with a prayer addressed to the Father, in the name of Jesus, and seeking the instruction and comfort of the Holy Spirit.

Before you dismiss:

- Remind group members to use the Scripture memory flash cards that are included in *Growing in Christ: becoming.*

- Say, "Next week, we'll discover some of the great events that make up the Church's history and see what we can learn from our past."

CHAPTER 5

Knowing God through His Story

Christian History

Focus

This chapter tells a story. In this session, you will track the growth, decline, and rebirth of the Christian church throughout history. Your group will come to understand that God is always at work through His church and that we can serve Him more effectively if we know His whole story—and our place in it.

Discovery: The church will always be God's chosen instrument for reaching the world.

Preparing

❏ Read chapter 5 of *Growing in Christ: becoming.*

❏ Review Matt. 16:13–19 and especially note the italicized phrases. You may want to consult a good study Bible before you discuss this passage.

❏ Review the Observing section of this lesson to identify the concepts that you will lead your group to discover.

❏ Choose an activity from "Icebreakers."

❏ Choose a teaching method from "Leader's Toolbox" that will help your group arrive at the discovery for this session.

❏ Choose a learning activity from "Memory Verse Learning Methods."

❏ Gather the materials you'll need for this session. Produce copies of the chart Turning Points in Christian History for your group. Be prepared to challenge the group to consider what might be the next turning point in the history of the church.

❏ Pray that God will use this important lesson to move someone close to Him.

Hint: Personal testimony is an incredibly powerful teaching tool. Consider asking group members to share the story of how they came to be part of Christ's Church.

Suggested Object Lesson: A History Book

Coat the cover of the book with dust (or powder). Blow off the "dust" and say, "History doesn't have to be a dry subject. Today, we'll see that God has been at work in our world for a long time as we discover history—His story."

Suggested Songs

"Faith of Our Fathers" (Frederick W. Faber); "How Great Thou Art" (Carl Boberg); "Great Is Thy Faithfulness" (Thomas O. Chisolm); "Ancient of Days" (Gary Sadler & Jamie Harrill Harvill).

Connecting

Use the icebreaker to encourage group members to share with one another. Then take a minute to encourage group members to talk about how they are applying the lessons of *Building Faith* to their personal lives. Allow time for responses. Review prayer concerns from the last session and invite the group to share new requests for prayer. Lead the group in praying together.

Hint: The icebreaker can be a great way to introduce the subject of the session. Consider using an icebreaker that incorporates the theme of this chapter.

Discovering

Review the important Scriptures for this session, giving special attention to those portions in italics. The key verse is printed in bold. Before you begin, observe that genealogy is an increasingly popular hobby. Ask, "Why are people so interested in knowing where they came from?"

Matthew 16:13–19

¹³When Jesus came to the region of Caesarea Philippi, he asked his

disciples, "Who do people say the Son of Man is?" [14]They replied, "Some say John the Baptist; others say Elijah; and still others, Jeremiah or one of the prophets." [15]"But what about you?" he asked. *"Who do you say I am?"* [16]Simon Peter answered, *"You are the Christ, the Son of the living God."* [17]Jesus replied, "Blessed are you, Simon, son of Jonah, for this was not revealed to you by man, but by my Father in heaven. [18]**And I tell you that you are Peter, and** ***on this rock I will build my church***, **and the gates of Hades will not overcome it.** [19]I will give you the keys of the kingdom of heaven; whatever you bind on earth will be bound in heaven, and whatever you loose on earth will be loosed in heaven."

Invite the group to discuss these questions.

- What do these Scriptures tell you about the Church?

- On what does Jesus say He is building the Church?

If someone in your group has a Catholic background, he may suggest that Christ's words in Matthew mean that the church is built on Peter, whom Catholics call the first pope. Show the context of these verses by pointing out that the church is built on Peter's *confession of faith that Jesus is the Christ*, the long-awaited Messiah.

Memorizing

Lead your group in memorizing Matt. 16:18, using one of the activities from "Memory Verse Learning Methods." Encourage the group to review the memory verses between sessions by using the flash cards printed at the end of *Growing in Christ: becoming*.

Observing

The key points to observe in this session are:

- The four major eras of Christian history are Formation, Deformation, Reformation, and Transformation.

- Three major divisions of Christianity worldwide are Roman Catholic, Eastern Orthodox, and Protestant.

- The church is the worldwide fellowship of all believers, and is much larger than any local church.

- Evangelical Christians are committed to faithfully proclaiming the message of the Bible.

- The church needs to be revived continually.

Practicing

Ask the group, "What is the greatest need facing this congregation? What can you do to help meet it?"

Closing

End your session by reading the Apostles' Creed together, which may be found in the "Resources" section of this book.

Before you dismiss:

- Encourage group members to make use of the Personal Spiritual Journal pages included in each chapter of *Knowing Christ: believing*

- Say, "Next week, we'll find out more about some basic beliefs of the Christian faith."

CHAPTER 6

What Christians Believe

Doctrine

Focus

This session will help you group see why it is important to have correct, biblical beliefs. You will learn the basic Christian concepts concerning God, human beings, salvation, and the Christian life.

Discovery: What we believe affects the way we live.

Preparing

❏ Read chapter 6 of *Growing in Christ: becoming.*

❏ Review 1 Timothy 4:7–16 and 2 Peter 3:18, noting your insights.

❏ Review the Observing section of this lesson to identify the concepts that you will lead your group to discover.

❏ Choose an activity from "Icebreakers."

❏ Choose a teaching method from "Leader's Toolbox" that will help your group arrive at the discovery for this session.

❏ Choose a learning activity from "Memory Verse Learning Methods."

❏ Gather the materials you'll need for this session.

❏ Pray for each member of your group by name.

Hint: Some group members enjoy doing small learning assignments. Consider enlisting a group member to survey ten people on the question "Does what you believe about God affect how you treat people?" and share his or her findings as an introduction to this session.

Suggested Object Lesson: A Contract

Bring a marriage license, legal contract, or any other document that requires a signature. Say, "Before signing a contract, it's important to read the terms. The Bible states the terms of our covenant—our contract—with God."

Suggested Songs

"And Can it Be" (Charles Wesley); "O for a Thousand Tongues to Sing" (Charles Wesley); "The Church's One Foundation" (Samuel J. Stone).

Connecting

Use the icebreaker to encourage group members to share with one another. Then take a minute to encourage group members to talk about how they are applying the lessons of *Building Faith* to their personal lives. Allow time for responses. Review prayer concerns from the last session and invite the group to share new requests for prayer. Lead the group in praying together.

Hint: People love to be called by name. Greet each person by name as he or she arrives.

Discovering

Review the important Scriptures for this session, giving special attention to those portions in italics. The key verse is printed in bold. Before you begin, ask, "What is more important when you are building a bridge, theory or practice?"

1 Timothy 4:7–16

[7]Have nothing to do with *godless myths* and old wives' tales; rather, *train yourself to be godly.* [8]For physical training is of some value, but godliness has value for all things, holding promise for both the present life and the *life to come.* [9]This is a *trustworthy saying* that deserves full acceptance [10](and for this we labor and strive), that we *have put our hope in the living God,* who is *the Savior of all* men, and especially of those who believe. [11]Command and teach these things. [12]Don't let anyone look down on you *because you are young,* but *set an example* for the believers in *speech,* in *life,* in *love,* in *faith* and in

purity. [13]Until I come, *devote yourself to the public reading of Scripture*, to preaching and to teaching. [14]*Do not neglect your gift*, which was given you through a prophetic message when the body of elders laid their hands on you. [15]*Be diligent* in these matters; give yourself wholly to them, so that everyone may *see your progress.* [16]**Watch your life** and ***doctrine* closely. *Persevere in them*, because if you do, you will *save both yourself and your hearers.***

2 Peter 3:18

But *grow in the grace and knowledge of our Lord* and Savior Jesus Christ. To Him be glory both now and forever! Amen

Invite the group members to consider these questions either individually or in small groups.

- What do these Scriptures tell you about what you believe?

- In what ways are we to be examples to others?

- Why is it important to grow in such a way that others can see your progress?

- How can you know that what you believe is right?

Memorizing

Lead your group in memorizing 1 Tim. 4:16, using one of the activities from "Memory Verse Learning Methods." Consider offering a gift (perhaps a copy of *The Message* or some other translation of the Bible) to anyone who memorizes all of the key verses.

Observing

The key points to observe in this session are:

- A correct view of the Bible is important because that affects the way we live.

- God is both infinite and personal.

- Human beings have been corrupted by sin and need salvation.

- God offers salvation to all people, who may receive it by faith.

- God changes the heart of believers, empowering them to live holy lives.

- Christ is the head of the church, which exists to serve Him.

- In the end, believers in Christ will enjoy an eternal life in heaven.

Practicing

Before the class begins, ask group to write a brief paragraph (2–5 sentences) on the subject "What I Believe." Now ask, "How does what you think about God fit with what the Bible says?" Challenge the group to reexamine their beliefs and change them if necessary according to what the Bible teaches.

Closing

Bring your class to a close by offering a prayer, singing a song, or offering an affirmation and blessing.

Before you dismiss:

- Encourage your group members to maintain a daily time of prayer and Bible reading.

- Say, "Next week, you will learn how to study the Bible for yourself as we look at two of the greatest passages of Scripture."

Knowing Christ through His Word

Scripture

Focus

Two passages of Scripture, the Ten Commandments and the Sermon on the Mount, provide a foundation for the Christian life. They are a blueprint for being a Christian. As you examine these Scriptures, you'll discover that obeying God is largely a matter of *attitude*.

Discovery: Following Christ produces a change in the way I treat other people.

Preparing

❏ Read chapter 7 of *Growing in Christ: becoming*.

❏ Review Matt. 5:17–20, 6:33 and note your insights.

❏ Read the entire Sermon on the Mount (Matt. 5–7), noting your insights.

❏ Jot down your own notes about what portions of the Ten Commandments and the Sermon on the Mount would be most applicable to your students.

❏ Review the Observing section of this lesson to identify the concepts that you will lead your group to discover.

❏ Choose an activity from "Icebreakers."

❏ Choose a teaching method from "Leader's Toolbox" that will help your group arrive at the discovery for this session. You might want to plan a way to break your class into two small groups. Have the first group discuss the material on the Ten Commandments while the other examines the Beatitudes. Have each group share its insights with the entire class.

❑ Choose a learning activity from "Memory Verse Learning Methods."

❑ Prepare gifts for those who have memorized all key verses, if this is something that you have planned to do.

❑ Gather the materials you'll need for this session. Make copies of the chart on the Ten Commandments for students to complete in class.

❑ Pray about the prayer requests that have been mentioned recently in your group.

Hint: Current events make great attention getters. You may wish to gather recent newspaper or magazine articles that mention the Bible as a starter for this session.

Suggested Object Lesson: A Cup That's Dirty on the Inside

Say, "The cup looks clean from the outside, but looking inside shows a different story. Today we'll learn how to get clean from the inside out."

Suggested Songs

"Wonderful Words of Life" (Philip P. Bliss); "Standing on the Promises" (R. Kelso Carter); "Trust and Obey" (John H. Sammis).

Connecting

Use the icebreaker to encourage group members to share with one another. Then take a minute to encourage group members to talk about how they are applying the lessons of *Building Faith* to their personal lives. Allow time for responses. Review prayer concerns from the last session and invite the group to share new requests for prayer. Lead the group in praying together.

Hint: Use the Connecting time to help the group reflect on how they have grown by being part of this group. Ask, "What has the Lord taught you over the past several weeks?"

Discovering

Review the important Scriptures for this session, giving special attention to those portions in italics. The key verse is printed in bold. Before you begin, make the comment that the Bible is the best-selling book of all time. Ask, "Why do you think people care so much about the Bible, even those who don't take the time to read it?"

Matthew 5:17–20

[17]"Do not think that I have come to abolish the *Law or the Prophets*; I have not come to abolish them but *to fulfill them*. [18]I tell you the truth, until heaven and earth disappear, *not the smallest letter*, not the least stroke of a pen, will by any means *disappear from the Law* until everything is accomplished. [19]Anyone who breaks *one of the least of these commandments* and *teaches others to do the same* will be called *least in the kingdom* of heaven, but whoever *practices and teaches these commands* will be called *great in the kingdom* of heaven. [20]For I tell you that unless your righteousness surpasses that of the Pharisees and the teachers of the law, you will certainly not enter the kingdom of heaven."

Matthew 6:33

But *seek first his kingdom* and *his righteousness*, and all these things will be given to you as well.

Spend just a few moments reviewing the passage above and answering these questions:

- What do these verses tell you about God's Word?

- What is of the most importance based on these verses?

- In what ways do you influence others by how you live?

Memorizing

Lead your group in memorizing Matt. 6:33, using one of the activities from "Memory Verse Learning Methods." Remind the group to continue the habit of Scripture memorization even after this study has concluded. If you have chosen to do so, give gifts to those who have memorized all of the key verses for this study.

Observing

The key points to observe in this session are:

- The Ten Commandments show us how to display our love for God and others.

- The Beatitudes describe the attitudes and character of a disciple.

- Christians should be like "salt and light," having an influence on the world around them.

- Christians should do what is right and be humble, not expecting the praise of others.

- Christians should trust God first and not worry about other concerns of life.

Practicing

Ask your group members to reflect on this question: "Does my life look like the life described in the Sermon on the Mount?" Challenge them to identify one area of life that is not in harmony with the lifestyle represented in the Sermon on the Mount, then ask, "What can you do to make your life more like Christ?"

Closing

Close the session by praying that your group members will continue to grow strong in the faith.

Before you dismiss:

- Invite group members to continue their spiritual journey by joining a Sunday School class or small group.

- Encourage group members to continue learning with the next volume in the *Building Faith* series, *Reflecting Christ: being.*

Reflecting Christ

being

Session Plans

Reflecting Christ

Leader's Introduction

Reflecting Christ. What a worthy desire! It's an awesome privilege for a believer simply to reflect the glory of our Lord.

Unfortunately, many people are more focused on *doing* than on *being*. Since others usually judge us by our ability rather than our character, it's tempting to pour our energy into achievements at the neglect of spiritual vitality. Our culture has lost the true connection—the connection to God through His Son, Jesus Christ.

The neglect of the inner life has sad consequences. In a society that is driven by the need to succeed, many wink at the immoral lifestyles and corrupt practices of leaders. They believe that private life—being—has no connection to public life—doing. That deception is prevalent, in part, because of the belief that there is no absolute truth. Our culture questions whether truth exists, and, if it does, whether it's possible to live by it.

Absolute truth does exist! It is found in Jesus Christ. Jesus said, "I am the way and the truth and the life. No one comes to the Father except through me" (John 14:6). Living according to the truth must be the ultimate desire of every fully devoted follower of Christ. This is the goal of discipleship.

The purpose of this book, one in a series of books called *Building Faith,* is to help your students reconnect *being* with *doing* in life—to help them link the inner life of thoughts and beliefs with the outer life of relationships and actions. As your students read this book, they'll be challenged to learn more about Christ, to emulate His character, to reflect His holiness—to be Christlike.

Chapter one begins where many people have left off—with the question of control in their life. They will learn what it means to make Christ lord of their life, and they'll discover the joy of surrendering themselves completely to Him.

Most of us are searching for joy, fulfillment, and peace, often in the wrong places. The second chapter will direct them to the true source of contentment—the will of God. They'll learn that God has a plan for their life, and they'll learn how to pursue it.

If you were to offer a drink of water to someone who is thirsty, would it make any difference in the world? Yes, it would. As followers of Jesus Christ, we are interested in meeting the ever-present social needs of our world. Chapter three explains why social action is important for every believer.

Leadership is a buzzword these days. Nearly everyone has a plan for motivating and directing other people. Yet Jesus calls us to be servants. In chapter four they'll discover that we reflect Christ best by becoming *servant leaders.*

The Bible teaches that the family is a reflection of the church. Today, powerful forces tear constantly at the basic unit of society—the family. The fifth chapter helps us to understand the value of the family, and our place in it.

To aid us in living holy lives, we explore two important Bible passages in chapter six: the Twenty-third Psalm and John chapters 14–17. These Pivotal scriptures explain God's relationship with His people and Jesus' relationship with His followers. Through them, we'll learn the basic ways in which we reflect Christ.

Suffering! What can I learn from that? In fact, suffering is an unavoidable part of life and can be a valuable learning experience. In chapter seven they'll gain a fresh perspective on this universal experience.

The final chapter takes us into the battle—spiritual battle with the Enemy. Our understanding of the spiritual affects our very being. Who is the Enemy? How can we have victory? We'll find out in this vital chapter.

As students learn from this book, there is a tool that will help them put it all together—the *Building Faith* Chart. (You'll find it in the Introduction.) They will see that there are ten important truths that form the foundation of every disciple's life. These truths are woven throughout this book. To help them connect these important principles to their life—and to show them how they function in the church—we've summarized them in the *Building Faith* Chart. You'll want to refer your students to it often.

—Ray E. Barnwell, Sr.

Giving Up without a Fight

The Lordship of Christ

Focus

Many people resist surrendering their lives completely to Christ. While they believe they are fully obedient to Him, their lifestyles may reveal a divided allegiance, particularly where money is concerned. In this session, you will move beyond knowing Jesus as Savior only and come to own Him as Lord or Master of all of life.

Discovery: Christians have dual citizenship—on earth and in heaven.

Preparing

❏ Read chapter 1 of *Reflecting Christ: being*.

❏ Review Matt. 6:24; John 1:1–3, 11:27; Rom. 13:14; Col. 1:15–20; and Phil. 3:20–21, noting your insights.

❏ Review the Observing section of this lesson to identify the concepts that you will lead your group to discover.

❏ Choose an activity from "Icebreakers."

❏ Choose a teaching method from "Leader's Toolbox" that will help your group arrive at the discovery for this session.

❏ Choose a learning activity from "Memory Verse Learning Methods."

❏ Gather the materials you'll need for this session.

❏ Pray that God will use this study to transform lives.

Hint: Remember to vary your teaching methods from week to week. You can also use more than one method in a single session.

Suggested Object Lesson: A Cardboard Crown

Pass the crown around and invite each person to try it on. Ask, "How would it feel to be a king or queen? Today, we'll talk about who is the king of your life."

Suggested Songs

"He Is Lord" (Unknown); "We Bow Down" (Twila Paris); "O to Be Like Thee" (Thomas O. Chisholm); "Jesus Is Lord of All" (William Gaither).

Connecting

Greet each member of your group and welcome off of them to the *Building Faith* series. Explain that the purpose of these sessions is to *help believers grow* in their new life in Christ.

People need to warm up to each other before they'll share the important things in their lives, so use one or more icebreaker activities to encourage relationship building.

If this group has met before and has already established relationships, continue the sharing, caring, and prayer time, using a variety of approaches.

If this is a new group, tell them that *prayer, caring, and sharing* each other's concerns will be an important part of what you do together. Invite group members to share:

- Praise Items—Good things that God has done in their lives lately

- Prayer Requests—Concerns for themselves or for a friend

- Needs—Things in their lives or in the community that the group might be able to help with

Consider enlisting someone to record prayer requests and praise items for the group each week—that will help you remember to pray consistently for important needs and celebrate answers to prayer.

Lead the group in a time of prayer. Remember, there are lots of ways for a group to pray together. See the "Leader's Toolbox" for some ideas.

Discovering

Review the important Scriptures for this session, giving special attention to those portions in italics. The key verse is printed in bold. Before you begin, ask, "Who is in charge of your life?"

Matthew 6:24

No one can serve *two masters*. Either he will *hate the one* and *love the other*, or he will be devoted to the one and despise the other.

John 1:1–3

[1]In the beginning was *the Word*, and the Word was with God, and the W*ord was God*. [2]He was with God in the beginning. [3]Through him *all things were made*; without him nothing was made that has been made.

John 11:27

"Yes, Lord," she told Him, "I believe that *you are the Christ*, the Son of God, who was to come into the world."

Romans 13:14

Rather, *clothe yourselves with the Lord Jesus Christ*, and *do not think about* how to gratify the desires of the sinful nature.

Colossians 1:15–20

[15]He is the *image of the invisible God*, the firstborn over all creation. [16]For by him all things were created: things in heaven and on earth, visible and invisible, whether thrones or powers or rulers or authorities; all things were created by him and for him. [17]He is before all things, and *in him all things hold together*. [18]And he is the head of the body, the church; he is the beginning and the firstborn from among the dead, so that *in everything he might have the supremacy*. [19]For God was pleased to have *all his fullness* dwell in him, [20]and through him to *reconcile to himself* all things, whether things on earth or things in heaven, by making peace through his blood, shed on the cross.

Philippians 3:20–21

[20]**But our *citizenship is in heaven*. And we eagerly await a Savior from there, the Lord Jesus Christ, [21]who, by *the power that enables him* to bring everything under his control, will *transform* our lowly bodies so that they will *be like his glorious body*.**

Ask group members to write down their answers to these questions, then share their responses with the group.

- What do these Scriptures tell you about Jesus' role in creation?

- What do these Scriptures tell you about Jesus' role in your life?

- What does it mean that Jesus is Lord?

Memorizing

Lead your group in memorizing Phil. 3:20–21, using one of the activities from "Memory Verse Learning Methods." Encourage the group to review the memory verses between sessions by using the flash cards printed at the end of *Reflecting Christ: being.* You may also want to encourage them to memorize by offering a gift to everyone who memorizes all the verses.

Observing

The key points to observe in this session are:

- Jesus Christ is Lord over all of creation.

- Jesus must be Lord over each Christian's life.

- You must acknowledge Jesus as Lord by an act of your will.

- When Jesus is Lord, your life will change for the better.

Practicing

Challenge group members to examine their recent behavior and ask: "Do these actions reflect the 'old' person that I was or the 'new' person that Jesus made me?"

Closing

Challenge your class to make a decision about the Lordship of Christ. Offer an opportunity for them to acknowledge that Jesus is Lord. Pray for those who are at the point of making this decision.

Before you dismiss:

- Remind group members to bring a Bible to each session.

- Ask, "Does God have a plan for your life? Find out in our next session."

CHAPTER 2

A Wonderful Plan for Your Life

God's Will

Focus

God has a general will for all people (that they should be saved) as well as a specific will for each individual. This session will help group members discover God's will for their lives.

Discovery: God has a plan for me.

Preparing

❏ Read chapter 2 of *Reflecting Christ: being.*

❏ Review Rom. 12:1–2 and Col. 4:12, noting your personal insights.

❏ Review the Observing section of this lesson to identify the concepts that you will lead your group to discover.

❏ Choose an activity from "Icebreakers."

❏ Choose a teaching method from "Leader's Toolbox" that will help your group arrive at the discovery for this session. Consider using questions to arouse interest in the subject, such as: Have you ever heard someone tell an amazing story regarding the revelation of God's will in their life? Who was it and what happened? Do you think God works like that today?

❏ Choose a learning activity from "Memory Verse Learning Methods."

❏ Gather the materials you'll need for this session.

❏ Pray for each member of your group by name.

Hint: Some group members may be more comfortable writing their reactions than speaking aloud in class.

Suggested Object Lesson: A Floor Plan

Say, "When you build, you need a plan. Today we begin to discover God's plan for our lives."

Suggested Songs

"Have Thine Own Way" (Adelaide A. Pollard); "All to Jesus I Surrender" (Judson W. VanDeventer); "Yes, Lord, Yes" (Unknown); "Step by Step" (Beaker).

Connecting

Use an icebreaker activity to encourage relationship building.

As a follow-up of the discussion in the last session, you might invite one or two group members to tell about making Christ lord of their life.

Invite group members to share:

- Praise Items—Good things that God has done in their lives lately

- Prayer Requests—Concerns for themselves or for a friend

- Needs—Things in their lives or in the community that the group might be able to help with

Review prayer requests from the last session, and lead the group in a time of prayer. Remember, there are lots of ways for a group to pray together. See the "Leader's Toolbox" for some ideas.

Discovering

Review the important Scriptures for this session, giving special attention to those portions in italics. The key verse is printed in bold. Before you begin, ask, "Are you doing what God wants you to do with your life? How do you know?"

Romans 12:1–2

¹**Therefore, I urge you, brothers, in view of God's mercy, to offer your bodies as living sacrifices, holy and pleasing to God—this is your spiritual act of worship. ²Do not conform any longer to the pattern of this world, but be transformed by the renewing of your mind. Then you will be able to test and approve what God's will is—his good, pleasing and perfect will.**

Colossians 4:12

> Epaphras, who is one of you and a servant of Christ Jesus, sends greetings. He is always wrestling in prayer for you, that you may stand firm in all the will of God, mature and fully assured.

Direct the group members to read Romans 12:1–2. Ask them to read the passage and comment on what happens to us before we are able to "test and approve what God's will is."

Memorizing

Spend a few minutes helping your group learn or review the memory verse using one of the Scripture memory options. Remind them that all the memory verses are printed on cards at the back of the book.

Observing

Key points for discussion are:

- God's general will for all people is that they should be saved.

- We seek God's specific will for our lives by prayer, the guidance of the Holy Spirit, advice from others, and reason.

- God calls some people to serve Him in full-time Christian ministry.

- We are in danger of missing God's will for our lives when we disobey Him.

Practicing

Ask group members to draw a timeline of their lives from birth to the present and mark the moments when God revealed Himself to them in some way. Ask for volunteers to tell how God has revealed His specific will for their lives.

Closing

Close the session by praying the Lord's Prayer as a group.
Before you dismiss:

- Encourage group members to make use of the Personal Spiritual Journal pages included in each chapter of *Reflecting Christ: being*.

- Say, "Next week, we'll talk about meeting the needs of people in our community and the world."

CHAPTER 3

A Cup of Cold Water

Social Issues

Focus

This session will challenge believers to move beyond their fear or prejudice and offer compassionate help to hurting people in their community. You'll identify some of the reasons that we resist showing compassion on others, and you'll come to see why it is so important that we do so.

Discovery: Compassion is love in action.

Preparing

❑ Read chapter 3 of *Reflecting Christ: being.*

❑ Review Matt. 25:31–40 and 1 John 3:17–18 and note your personal insights.

❑ Review the Observing section of this lesson to identify the concepts that you will lead your group to discover.

❑ Choose an activity from "Icebreakers."

❑ Choose a teaching method from "Leader's Toolbox" that will help your group arrive at the discovery for this session.

❑ Research some ways that your group might meet a need for others. Some ways they might do that are by providing care packages for a children's home or prison inmates; collecting canned goods for a local food pantry; doing clean-up and light repair work in the home of a single parent or a widow; putting on a clothing drive for a local social service agency.

❑ Choose a learning activity from "Memory Verse Learning Methods."

❏ Gather the materials you'll need for this session.

❏ Pray for your spiritual growth as you lead others in *Building Faith.*

Hint: Many people are visual learners. Consider using a prop or visual aid in this session.

Suggested Object Lesson: A Cup of Water

Distribute a cup of cold water to each person and ask, "What is a small thing you might do to help someone in need? Even if it's just a cup of water, we are responsible to show compassion to those in need."

Suggested Songs

"Song for the Nations" (Chris Chistensen); "People Need the Lord" (Steve Green); "Shine, Jesus, Shine" (Graham Kendrick).

Connecting

Use the icebreaker to encourage group members to share with one another. Then take a minute to encourage group members to talk about how they are applying the lessons of *Building Faith* to their personal lives. Allow time for responses. Review prayer concerns from the last session and invite the group to share new requests for prayer. Lead the group in praying together.

Hint: Remember that group interaction begins prior to the session itself. That's why room arrangement is important and a circle arrangement for seating is often best.

Discovering

Review the important Scriptures for this session, giving special attention to those portions in italics. The key verse is printed in bold. Consider inviting three group members to perform a dramatic reading of the Matthew passage. The parts could be the Narrator, the King, and the Sheep.

Matthew 25:31–40

³¹"When *the Son of Man* comes in his glory, and all the angels with him, he will sit on his throne in heavenly glory. ³²All the nations will be gathered before him, and *he will separate the people* one from another as a shepherd separates the sheep from the goats. ³³He will

put the sheep on his right and the goats on his left. [34]"Then the King will say to those on his right, 'Come, *you who are blessed* by my Father; take your *inheritance*, the kingdom prepared for you since the creation of the world. [35]For I was *hungry* and *you gave me something to eat*, I was *thirsty* and *you gave me something to drink*, I was a *stranger* and *you invited me in*, [36]I *needed clothes* and *you clothed me*, I was *sick* and *you looked after me*, I was *in prison* and *you came to visit me*.' [37]"Then the righteous will answer him, 'Lord, *when did we see you* hungry and feed you, or thirsty and give you something to drink? [38]When did we see you a stranger and invite you in, or needing clothes and clothe you? [39]When did we see you sick or in prison and go to visit you?' [40]"The King will reply, 'I tell you the truth, *whatever you did* for one of the *least* of these brothers of mine, *you did for me*.'"

1 John 3:17–18

If anyone has *material possessions* and sees his brother *in need* but has *no pity* on him, how can the love of God be in him? Dear children, let us not *love* with words or tongue but *with actions and in truth*.

Ask group members to work in pairs or triads as they respond to these questions.

- What will bring God's commendation according to these verses?

- In what ways should we do the things that these verses suggest: feed the hungry, clothe the needy, visit the sick and imprisoned?

- Who are we really serving when we serve the needy?

- What should be our motive in serving those in need?

Memorizing

Lead your group in memorizing 1 John 3:17–18, using one of the activities from "Memory Verse Learning Methods." Remind group members that memorizing God's Word builds their strength to resist temptation and helps them make choices that please God.

Observing

The key points to observe in this session are:

- Compassion is love in action.

- Caring for others is one way of being "salt and light" in the world.

- Compassionate action should be undertaken intelligently.

- We must overcome fear to reach out to others.

Practicing

Present one or two ideas for compassionate action that the group might be able to undertake. Challenge the group to form a plan and take action!

Closing

Bring the session to a close by praying that God will lay a burden on each person's heart to live as salt and light in the world.

Before you dismiss:

- Remind group members to pray for one another during the week.

- Ask, "What are the characteristics of a good leader? We'll find out in our next session."

CHAPTER 4

The Last Shall Be First

Servant Leadership

Focus

Through this session, your group will gain a correct understanding of what it means to be a leader. *Servant leadership* involves self-discipline, submission to spiritual authority, and cooperating with others in body of Christ. Servant leadership can only be sustained through accountability to God and others.

Discovery: Leaders must be self-disciplined and under the authority of God before they can lead others.

Preparing

❏ Read chapter 4 of *Reflecting Christ: being.*

❏ Review Matt. 20:25–28 and note your insights.

❏ Review the Observing section of this lesson to identify the concepts that you will lead your group to discover.

❏ Choose an activity from "Icebreakers."

❏ Choose a teaching method from "Leader's Toolbox" that will help your group arrive at the discovery for this session.

❏ Choose a learning activity from "Memory Verse Learning Methods."

❏ Gather the materials you'll need for this session.

❏ Ask the Holy Spirit to give you wisdom for communicating his truth.

Hint: Everyone can use a little encouragement. E-mail or call your group members during the week to tell them that you appreciate their participation in *Building Faith.*

Suggested Object Lesson: A Serving Tray

Ask, "Name some symbols of leadership. Do you think that someone who waits on the needs of others could be a leader? We'll find out today."

Suggested Songs

"I Will Serve Thee" (William Gaither); "All Hail, King Jesus" (Dave Moody); "Take My Life and Let it Be" (Frances R. Havergal); "Sanctuary" (John Thompson and Randy Scruggs).

Connecting

Use the icebreaker to encourage group members to share with one another. Then take a minute to encourage group members to talk about how they are applying the lessons of *Building Faith* to their personal lives. Allow time for responses. Review prayer concerns from the last session and invite the group to share new requests for prayer. Lead the group in praying together.

Hint: Encourage group members to connect with one another during the week. Relationship building can take place outside the group meetings!

Discovering

Review the important Scriptures for this session, giving special attention to those portions in italics. The key verse is printed in bold. Before you begin, ask, "Who is the greatest leader in history? What made his or her leadership great?"

Matthew 20:25–28

[25]Jesus called them together and said, "You know that the rulers of the Gentiles lord it over them, and their high officials exercise authority over them. [26]**Not so with you. Instead, whoever wants to become great among you must be your servant,** [27]and whoever wants to be first must be your slave— [28]just as the Son of Man did not come to be served, but to serve, and to give his life as a ransom for many."

Ask everyone to write down their answers to these questions, then share their responses with the group.

- What do these Scriptures tell you about the way a leader should lead?

- In what ways do these verses confirm or conflict with society's view of leadership?

- In what ways do you see yourself as a leader?

Especially emphasize that believers lead by influence. They are influencing someone whether they realize it or not.

Memorizing

Using the memory option you selected, spend a few minutes helping your group learn or review the memory verse.

Observing

The key points to observe in this session are:

- Servant leadership involves self-leadership (leading inwardly), followership (leading under authority, and partnership (leading laterally).

- Effective leadership avoids the extremes of using others and pleasing others.

- Leaders are accountable in two directions:

    Vertical—to God
    Horizontal—to others

Practicing

Challenge group members to enter an accountability relationship. Ask them to think of a person whom they might ask to become an accountability partner, and encourage them to contact that person this week.

Closing

Bring your session to a close by praying that each group member will "finish well" in the Christian faith.

Before you dismiss:

- Remind group members to use the Scripture memory flash cards that are included in *Reflecting Christ: being.*

- Say, "Next week, we will discover that the family has been God's plan from the beginning."

CHAPTER 5

God's Plan from the Beginning

Family

Focus

This session is focused on the family. You'll come to understand why the marriage covenant is so important, get tips for creating a healthy marriage, and gain insight into raising godly children.

Discovery: God created gender, sexuality, and the family to provide for our needs.

Preparing

❏ Read chapter 5 of *Reflecting Christ: being*.

❏ Review Gen. 1:27–28 and Eph. 4:32–5:3 and note your insights.

❏ Review the Observing section of this lesson to identify the concepts that you will lead your group to discover.

❏ Choose an activity from "Icebreakers."

❏ Choose a teaching method from "Leader's Toolbox" that will help your group arrive at the discovery for this session.

❏ Choose a learning activity from "Memory Verse Learning Methods."

❏ Gather the materials you'll need for this session. Make copies of the list of questions titled Christian Family Values, found in the "Resources" section of this book.

❏ Pray that God will use this important lesson to move someone close to Him.

Hint: A visiting expert adds interest to any subject. Consider inviting someone with expertise on family matters to meet with your class (such as a pastor, counselor, or social worker).

Suggested Object Lesson: Pictures of Several Families

Ask the group to share memories of their family experiences. Say, "Family is one of the most important things in our lives. The family was created by God. Let's learn how to keep our families strong."

Suggested Songs

"The Family Prayer Song—As For Me and My House" (Morris Chapman); "Savior, Like a Shepherd Lead Us" (Dorothy A. Thrupp); "Gentle Shepherd" (William Gaither).

Connecting

Use the icebreaker to encourage group members to share with one another. Allow a "testimony time," when group members are encouraged to talk about how they are applying the lessons of *Building Faith* to their personal lives. Review prayer concerns from the last session and invite the group to share new requests for prayer. Lead the group in praying together.

Hint: The icebreaker can be a great way to introduce the subject of the session. Consider using an icebreaker that incorporates the theme of this chapter.

Discovering

Review the important Scriptures for this session, giving special attention to those portions in italics. The key verse is printed in bold. Before you begin, ask, "Why is it so hard for families to stay together these days?"

Genesis 1:27, 28

[27]So God created man in *his own image*, in the image of God he created him; *male and female he created them.* [28]*God blessed them* and said to them, *"Be fruitful and increase* in number; fill the earth and subdue it. *Rule* over the fish of the sea and the birds of the air and over every living creature that moves on the ground."

Ephesians 4:32–5:3

> [32]*Be kind and compassionate to one another,* *forgiving* each other, just as in Christ God forgave you. [1]Be *imitators of God*, therefore, as dearly loved children [2]**and** *live a life of love***, just as Christ loved us and gave himself up for us as a fragrant offering and sacrifice to God.** [3]But among you *there must not be even a hint of sexual immorality*, or of any kind of *impurity*, or of *greed*, because these are *improper for God's holy people*.

Divide the group into smaller groups (of two or three each) to discuss a few of the questions listed on the Christian Family Values Questions for Reflection Sheet found in the "Resources" section of this book. Reassemble as a larger group and ask:

- What does it mean to be created in the image of God?

- What commands did God give the first humans? Do those commands still apply to us today?

- What are the characteristics of God's holy people?

- Why does the verse in Ephesians 5:3 specifically name sexual immorality, impurity, and greed?

Memorizing

Lead your group in memorizing Eph. 5:2, using one of the activities from "Memory Verse Learning Methods." Encourage the group to review the memory verses between sessions by using the flash cards printed at the end of *Reflecting Christ: being*.

Observing

The key points to observe in this session are:

- God created the family and sexuality.

- The marriage covenant is the foundation of the family.

- Love, respect, responsibility, and mutual submission are key elements of marriage.

- Children need love, training, and a good example to follow.

Practicing

Ask class members to identify one area of their family life that needs to be strengthened. Possible responses include communication with a spouse, time spent with children, child discipline, and faithfulness in marriage. Ask, "What will you do this week to improve that area of your family life?"

Closing

Bring your class to a close by asking each group member to write a note to a family member that begins, "I will show you that I love you by. . . ."

Before you dismiss:

- Encourage group members to make use of the Personal Spiritual Journal pages included in each chapter of *Reflecting Christ: being*.

- Ask, "How do you know that God loves you? Two key passages of the Bible will give us the answer in the next session."

CHAPTER 6

Beside Still Waters

Key Passages from the Bible

Focus

This session explores the nature of our relationship with God by examining two important Scriptures, the Shepherd's Psalm (Psalm 23) and the High Priestly Prayer of Jesus (John 13–17). You'll discover that God wants to meet our needs for companionship and love. Our response to His love is to love Him in return and to obey him.

Discovery: God loves you.

Preparing

❏ Consider treating this material into two sessions—Psalm 23 for the first and John 13–17 for the second.

❏ Read chapter 6 of *Reflecting Christ: being.*

❏ Review Psalm 23 and John 13–17, and note your insights. Recall how these passages may have influenced your own walk with God. Recall the lives of people you have known who seemed to embody the concepts found in these Scriptures.

❏ Review the Observing section of this lesson to identify the concepts that you will lead your group to discover.

❏ Choose an activity from "Icebreakers."

❏ Choose a teaching method from "Leader's Toolbox" that will help your group arrive at the discovery for this session.

❏ Choose a learning activity from "Memory Verse Learning Methods."

❏ Gather the materials you'll need for this session. Consider making copies (with permission) of the hymn "The Lord Is My Shepherd" or another Christian song that is based on Psalm 23.

❑ Pray for each member of your group by name.

Hint: Some group members enjoy doing small learning assignments. Consider enlisting a group member to help with presenting this session.

Suggested Object Lesson: Oil for Anointing

Explain that oil is considered a sign of richness. The oil signifies God's abundant supply. You may wish to anoint each person in your group and pray for him or her.

Suggested Songs

"Love Divine, All Love Excelling" (Charles Wesley); "Trust and Obey" (John H. Sammis); "Thy Word Is a Lamp unto My Feet" (Michael W. Smith); "As the Deer—Psalm 42:1" (Martin Nystrom).

Connecting

Use the icebreaker to encourage group members to share with one another. Allow a "testimony time," when group members are encouraged to talk about how they are applying the lessons of *Building Faith* to their personal lives. Review prayer concerns from the last session and invite the group to share new requests for prayer. Lead the group in praying together.

Hint: People love to be called by name. Greet each person by name as he or she arrives.

Discovering

Review the important Scriptures for this session, giving special attention to those portions in italics. The key verse is printed in bold. Have group members share their responses to the exercises on pages 103 and 107 of *Reflecting Christ: being*.

Psalm 23:1–6

Stanza One

¹The LORD is my shepherd, I shall not be in want.
²ᵃHe makes me lie down in green pastures,
²ᵇhe leads me beside quiet waters,
³ᵃhe restores my soul.

[3b]He guides me in paths of righteousness

[3c]for his name's sake.

[4a,b]Even though I walk through the valley of the shadow of death

[4c]I will fear no evil.

Centering line

[4d]for you are with me,

[4e]your rod and your staff,

[4f]they comfort me.

Stanza two

[5a]You prepare a table before me

[5b]in the presence of my enemies.

[5c]You anoint my head with oil;

[5d]my cup overflows.

[6a]Surely goodness and love will follow me

[6b]all the days of my life,

[6c]and I will dwell in the house of the LORD

[6d]forever.

John 15:9

As the Father has loved me, so have I loved you. Remain in my love."

Ask group members to write down their answers to these questions, then share their responses with the group.

- What do these Scriptures tell you about the way God cares for you?

- In what ways do these verses bring comfort to those who are sad or discouraged?

- How has God comforted you?

Memorizing

Lead your group in memorizing John 15:19, using one of the activities from "Memory Verse Learning Methods." Consider offering a gift (perhaps a copy of *The Message* or some other translation of the Bible) to anyone who memorizes all of the key verses.

Observing

The key points to observe in Psalm 23 are:

- God provides for us "I shall not be in want".

- God protects us ("I will fear no evil).

- God guarantees our future ("I will dwell in the house of the LORD forever").

The key points to observe in John 13–17 are:

- Father, Son, and Holy Spirit are united in wanting an intimate relationship with believers.

- God is our source, our redeemer, and our companion; thus we are equipped for any situation.

Practicing

Encourage group members to practice the presence of God this week in one of the following ways:

- Force yourself to slow down for five minutes on a stressful day and let God speak to you.

- Listen patiently to the questions asked by your family and friends.

- Fast for one meal and spend time listening to God.

- Meditate on Psalm 23.

Closing

Close your session with prayer. As you begin, ask group members to breathe deeply and remember that God is their breath or spirit. Then give group members the opportunity to use their breath to put their concerns and thanksgiving into words.

Before you dismiss:

- Encourage your group members to maintain a daily time of prayer and Bible reading.

- Say, "Next week, we will look at the hard lessons that suffering brings and learn that God enables us to cope with it."

CHAPTER 7

The Hardest Lesson

Suffering

Focus

This session explores the reason for and the best reactions to suffering. You'll discover that God cares deeply about the suffering of His creation, and you'll learn that we can cope with pain by trusting God, focusing on things of eternal value, and seeking appropriate help.

Discovery: I can grow stronger spiritually when I suffer physically.

Preparing

❏ Read chapter 7 of *Reflecting Christ: being*.

❏ Review Job 36:15; 1 Peter 4:12–16; 2 Corinthians 1:3–7, and note your personal insights.

❏ Review the Observing section of this lesson to identify the concepts that you will lead your group to discover.

❏ Choose an activity from "Icebreakers."

❏ Choose a teaching method from "Leader's Toolbox" that will help your group arrive at the discovery for this session.

❏ Choose a learning activity from "Memory Verse Learning Methods."

❏ Gather the materials you'll need for this session.

❏ Pray about the prayer requests that have been mentioned recently in your group.

Hint: Current events make great attention getters. You may wish to gather recent news stories that deal with suffering as a starter for this session.

Suggested Object Lesson: A Box of Bandages

Ask each person to take a bandage from the box. Ask, "What does it take to deal with pain? How big a bandage does it take to heal the soul?"

Suggested Songs

"He Giveth More Grace" (Annie Johnson Flint); "God Will Make a Way" (Janet Paschal); "It Is Well With My Soul" (Henry G. Spafford).

Connecting

Use the icebreaker to encourage group members to share with one another. Allow a "testimony time," when group members are encouraged to talk about how they are applying the lessons of *Building Faith* to their personal lives. Review prayer concerns from the last session and invite the group to share new requests for prayer. Lead the group in praying together.

Hint: People who are unwilling to pray in a large group may be willing to pray in a group of two or three.

Discovering

Review the important Scriptures for this session, giving special attention to those portions in italics. The key verse is printed in bold. Before you begin, ask, "What is the worst thing that can happen to a person?"

Job 36:15

> But *those who suffer* he *delivers* in their suffering; he *speaks* to them *in their affliction.*

2 Corinthians 1:3–7

> ³Praise be to the God and Father of our Lord Jesus Christ, the *Father of compassion* and the *God of all comfort*, ⁴who comforts us in all our troubles, so that *we can comfort* those in any trouble with the comfort we ourselves have received from God. ⁵For just as the *sufferings of Christ* flow over into our lives, so also *through Christ our comfort overflows.* ⁶If we are distressed, it is for your comfort and salvation; if we are comforted, it is for your comfort, which

produces in you *patient endurance* of the same sufferings we suffer. [7]And our hope for you is firm, because we know that just as you *share in our sufferings*, so also you *share in our comfort*.

1 Peter 4:12–16

[12]Dear friends, *do not be surprised at the painful trial* you are suffering, as though something strange were happening to you. [13]But rejoice that you participate in *the sufferings of Christ*, so that you may be overjoyed when his glory is revealed. [14]If you are insulted because of the name of Christ, you are blessed, for the Spirit of glory and of God rests on you. [15]If you suffer, it should not be as a murderer or thief or any other kind of criminal, or even as a meddler. [16]However, *if you suffer as a Christian, do not be ashamed*, but praise God that you bear that name.

Ask group members to share their responses to these questions:

- What do these Scriptures tell you about suffering?

- What do they tell you about comfort in suffering?

- In what ways do these verses give you hope? Warning?

- What do you learn about Christ in these passages?

Memorizing

Lead your group in memorizing Job 36:15, using one of the activities from "Memory Verse Learning Methods." Encourage the group to review the memory verses between sessions by using the flash cards printed at the end of *Reflecting Christ: being*. If you have chosen this option, remind them that you will present a gift to each person who memorizes all of the key verses for this study series.

Observing

The key points to observe in this session are:

- Pain may have several causes, including physical, spiritual, and emotional trauma.

- Since Jesus and many of His followers suffered, we know that we will not be exempt from suffering.

- Pain has the positive value of helping us identify the source of a problem.

- Unwise choices bring needless suffering.

- We cope with pain by trusting God, focusing on things of eternal value, and seeking appropriate help.

Practicing

Ask group members to identify one or two people they know who are suffering. Ask, "What action could you—or we as a group—take to comfort one of these people who are suffering?"

Closing

Bring your class to a close by offering a prayer, singing a song, or offering an affirmation and blessing.

Before you dismiss:

- Remind group members to keep in touch during the week by phone or E-mail, and to pray for one another.

- Ask, "Does it feel as if every day of your life is a battle? Next week, we'll learn how to prepare for spiritual warfare."

CHAPTER 8

Battling the Devil

Spiritual Warfare

Focus

Spiritual warfare is a real thing. This session helps believers identify the spiritual battlegrounds in their lives—self, home, community, and church—and to prepare themselves to face them.

Discovery: Jesus has already won the victory over Satan.

Preparing

❏ Read chapter 8 of *Reflecting Christ: being.*

❏ Review Eph. 6:10–18 and note your insights.

❏ Review the Observing section of this lesson to identify the concepts that you will lead your group to discover.

❏ Choose an activity from "Icebreakers."

❏ Choose a teaching method from "Leader's Toolbox" that will help your group arrive at the discovery for this session.

❏ Review recent events in your community that may be an indication of spiritual warfare. You might speak with lawyers, policemen, social workers, or alcohol and drug abuse counselors to learn about the problems in your community.

❏ Choose a learning activity from "Memory Verse Learning Methods."

❏ Gather the materials you'll need for this session.

❏ Prepare gifts for those who have memorized all key verses, if this is something that you have planned to do.

❏ Pray for your group as they continue to grow in the faith.

Hint: Experience is a powerful learning tool. If circumstances permit, you might take a field trip to a jail, hospital, or substance abuse treatment center.

Suggested Object Lesson: Toy Soldiers

Ask, "What battleground is most active in your life today? How do you recognize the Enemy? How do you deal with the Enemy?"

Suggested Songs

"What A Mighty God We Serve" (Unknown); "Praise the Name of Jesus" (Roy Hicks, Jr.); "The Name of the Lord" (Clinton Utterbach); "Victory in Jesus" (Eliza E. Hewitt).

Connecting

Use the icebreaker to encourage group members to share with one another. Allow a "testimony time," when group members are encouraged to talk about how they are applying the lessons of *Building Faith* to their personal lives. Review prayer concerns from the last session and invite the group to share new requests for prayer. Lead the group in praying together.

Hint: Use the Connecting time to help the group reflect on how they have grown by being part of this group. Ask, "What has the Lord taught you over the past several weeks?"

Discovering

Review the important Scriptures for this session, giving special attention to those portions in italics. The key verse is printed in bold. Before you begin, ask, "Is the Devil a real being?"

Ephesians 6:10–18

[10]Finally, *be strong in the Lord* and in his mighty power. [11]*Put on the full armor of God* so that you can take your stand against the devil's schemes. [12]**For our struggle is not against flesh and blood, but** *against the rulers*, **against the** *authorities*, **against the** *powers of this dark world* **and against the** *spiritual forces of evil* **in the heavenly realms.** [13]Therefore put on the full armor of God, so that when the day of evil comes, you may be able to *stand your ground*,

and after you have done everything, to stand. [14]Stand firm then, with the *belt of truth* buckled around your waist, with the *breastplate of righteousness* in place, [15]and with your *feet fitted* with the readiness that comes from the *gospel of peace*. [16]In addition to all this, take up the *shield of faith*, with which you can extinguish all the flaming arrows of the evil one. [17]Take the *helmet of salvation* and the *sword of the Spirit*, which is the word of God. [18]And *pray* in the Spirit on all occasions with all kinds of prayers and requests. With this in mind, be alert and always *keep on praying* for all the saints.

Ask the group to share their responses about what it means to be in a spiritual battle.

- How do we recognize the Enemy?

- How do we fight if we're not fighting against flesh and blood?

- What is included in our spiritual armor and how do we use it?

- What special protection is there in praying for each other?

Memorizing

Lead your group in memorizing Eph. 6:12, using one of the activities from "Memory Verse Learning Methods." Remind the group to continue the habit of Scripture memorization even after this study has concluded. If you have chosen to do so, give gifts to those who have memorized all of the key verses for this study.

Observing

The key points to observe in this session are:

- Spiritual warfare is real.

- Spiritual battlegrounds include the home, forms of entertainment, substance abuse, and the occult.

- We can prepare ourselves for the battle by maintaining our spiritual, physical, and psychological health.

- We need not be afraid because God has already won the battle.

Practicing

Challenge group members to be aware of spiritual conflicts that they face during the week. Suggest that they keep a journal for one week, noting situations at home, work, school, or church that were indicators of a spiritual conflict or victory.

Closing

Bring your class to a close by offering a prayer, singing a song, or offering an affirmation and blessing. The group may want to spend a bit more time in prayer, thanking the Lord for their experience in this group.

Before you dismiss:

- Invite group members to continue their spiritual journey by joining a Sunday School class or small group.

- Encourage group members to continue learning growing in the faith.

Resources

Response Card

Realizing that the Bible teaches we should tithe, I will take this step of faith in God by committing the first 10 percent of my income to the Lord through this local church (the storehouse).

_____ I will begin tithing   _____ I already tithe

Name _____

Address _____

City, State, ZIP _____

Phone (home) _____(work) _____

_____ I need giving envelopes

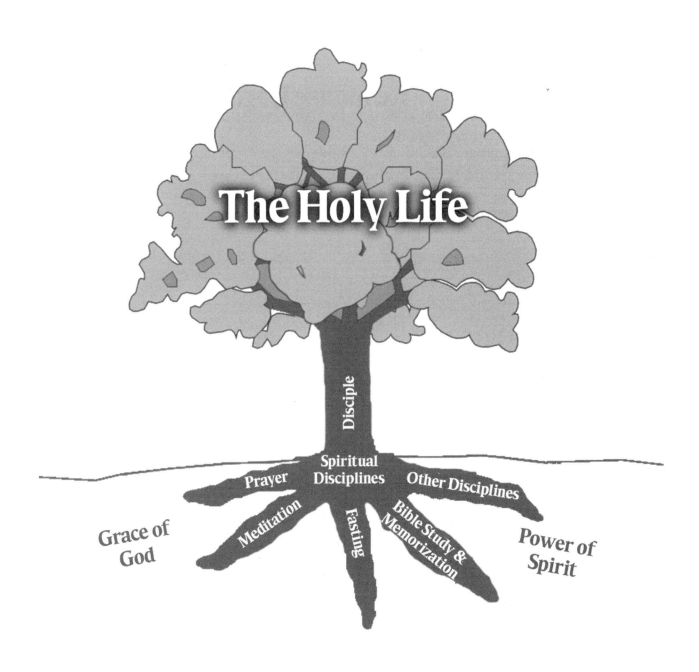

Bible Study Loop

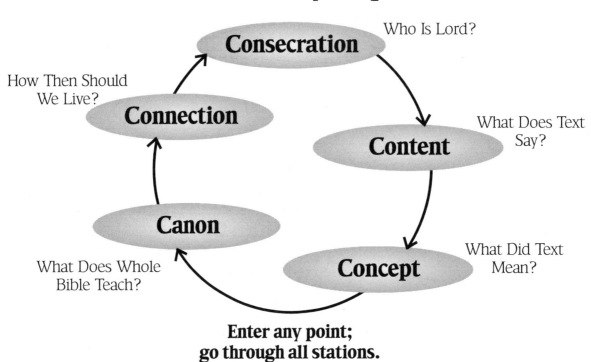

Consecration — Who Is Lord?

Content — What Does Text Say?

Concept — What Did Text Mean?

Canon — What Does Whole Bible Teach?

Connection — How Then Should We Live?

**Enter any point;
go through all stations.**

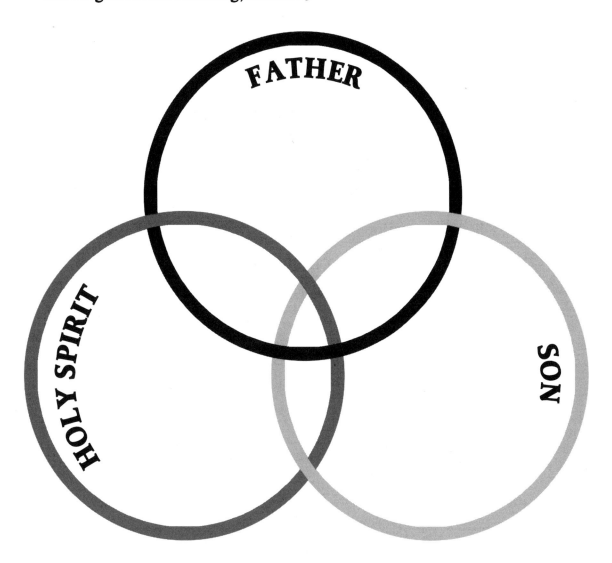

Compare These Old Testament and New Testament Passages.		
Old Testament	**New Testament**	**Comparison**
Isa. 6:5–10	Acts 28:25–27	
Exod. 17:7	Heb. 3:7–9	
Jer. 31:31–34	Heb. 10:15–17	

An Outline of Church History

The Formation of the Church (A.D. 30–500)

The Deformation of the Church (500–1500)

The Reformation of the Church (1500–1700)

The Transformation of the Church (1700–Present)

Branches of the Protestant Reformation

The Lutheran Church

The Reformed Churches

The Anabaptist Churches

The Church of England

Turning Points in Church History

A.D. 30   Pentecost: The Birthday of the Church

49–50   Jerusalem Conference opens the door for evangelization of the Gentiles

313   End of persecution as Christian emperor Constantine assumes power

325   Council of Nicea affirms deity of Christ

367   New Testament canon is recognized in final form

432   Patrick goes to Ireland as a missionary

732   Battle of Tours stops advance of Islam in Western Europe

1054   The Great Schism results in separation of Eastern Orthodox Church from Roman Catholic Church

1095   First Crusade is launched

1206   Francis of Assisi begins life of poverty

1380   John Wycliffe oversees first translation of Bible into English (approximate date)

1415   John Huss is burned at the stake

1517   Martin Luther posts *Ninety-Five Theses*

1521   Luther takes stand at Diet of Worms

1525   Anabaptist Movement begins

1534   Henry VIII declares himself head of the Church of England

1536   John Calvin publishes *Institutes of the Christian Religion*

1620   Puritan Pilgrims land at Plymouth Rock

1675   Philip Jacob Spener founds Pietist Movement

1738   Aldersgate experience of John Wesley

1740   High-water mark of the Great Awakening

1830   Charles Finney's revivals begin in Second Great Awakening

1906   Azusa Street Revival introduces Pentecostalism

1943   C. S. Lewis publishes *Mere Christianity*

1948   Mother Teresa begins mission in Calcutta, India

1949   Billy Graham gains national visibility with Los Angeles Crusade

1962   Vatican II Conference gives Catholicism new approach and attitude

The Apostles' Creed

I believe in God the Father Almighty, maker of heaven and earth:

And in Jesus Christ, His only Son, our Lord; who was conceived by the Holy Spirit, born of the Virgin Mary, suffered under Pontius Pilate, was crucified, dead, and buried; He descended into hades; The third day He rose again from the dead; He ascended into heaven, and sitteth at the right hand of God the Father Almighty; from thence He shall come to judge the living and the dead.

I believe in the Holy Spirit, the holy catholic church, the communion of saints, the forgiveness of sins, the resurrection of the body, and the life everlasting. Amen.

Christian Family Values
Questions for Reflection

1. Recall a video, movie or television program that you watched recently. What were the underlying values?

2. How can a couple reflect God's image more fully than one person?

3. What are some implications of God's blessing and approval on the Eden family unit?

4. How would you answer someone who asked, "What's wrong with living together?"

5. How can we keep from being influenced by the media's sexual values?

6. Name some specific ways that a husband and wife might share responsibilities.

7. What lessons—positive and negative—did you learn from your home of origin?

8. Give some examples of teachable moments for children in daily life.

9. What are some ways we might demonstrate values like kindness or unselfishness to children?

10. List some ways you can help the single parents in your church:

11. What are some helpful activities you can do to show Christian love to the young people of your church?

12. What are some other ministry projects you and your family can work on together?